THE PLACE-NAMES OF WESTERN GWENT

by GRAHAM OSBORNE
& GRAHAM HOBBS

Old Bakehouse Publications

Abertillery

First published in April 2002

ISBN 1 874538 59 X

Published in the U.K. by
Old Bakehouse Publications
Church Street,
Abertillery, Gwent NP13 1EA
Telephone: 01495 212600   Fax: 01495 216222
www.mediamaster.co.uk/oldbakebooks

Made and printed in the U.K.
by J.R. Davies (Printers) Ltd.

Dedication to Graham Hobbs

This volume is dedicated to Graham Hobbs the co-author of this work and of the companion volume *'The Place Names of Eastern Gwent'* which appeared in 1998.

Graham's sudden death in January 1998, was a shattering blow for his wife, family and many friends and to those familiar with his research on place-names. He was still comparatively young, still very full of enthusiasm for this topic and clearly capable of much more work. He will be missed most grievously but will be remembered with great affection.

Graham Hobbs

Graham Hobbs attended St. Illtyd's College, Cardiff. He then entered University College of Wales, Aberystwyth and after graduation proceeded to the University of Birmingham where he was awarded the degree of M.Sc. in Geology. He then worked for two years as a geologist in Antarctica and during this time Graham made a geological reconnaissance survey of the coast between Cape Murray and Cape Willems; Hobbs Point ($64^\circ37'$ S $163^\circ56'$ E) was subsequently named for him.

He joined the staff of St. Joseph's High School in Newport, becoming Head of Geology and Geography but with a short break in this service, during which time he worked as a geologist in Tasmania.

Graham was always a great enthusiast for the Welsh language and on retirement he was able to devote time to the study of the origins and meanings of Welsh place names, particularly those of Gwent/Monmouthshire. Some of this work is presented in this volume.

Graham also compiled an extensive list of name-forms of places in Gwent and was joint author of publications in the 'Gwent Local History Journal'. A keen rugby enthusiast he was also President of the Rugby Association at St. Joseph's.

Graham Osborne

Dr. Graham Osborne was born at Crosskeys and educated at the old Pontywaun Grammar School. After service with the Royal Signals in East Africa during the latter part of World War Two, he entered University College, Cardiff graduating with the degree of B.Sc. (1st Class Hons., Chemistry) before proceeding to a doctorate. He was then awarded a Research Fellowship at the University of Cambridge; at that time the molecular structure of DNA was being worked out. For six years he was a Senior Research Chemist in charge of a group of graduates working on organophosphorus insecticides at the Woodstock Agricultural Research Laboratories of 'Shell' Research.

A move to New Zealand then came, to the University of Canterbury, at first as lecturer in Organic Chemistry, then as Senior Lecturer in the Faculty of Agriculture.

He is the author of a large number of research publications on insecticides and on insect pheromones.

Local history had always been one of Graham Osborne's interests and with a return to Wales, on retirement, he was able to commence research in this field. A publication on the place-name 'Risca' soon appeared and in partnership with Graham Hobbs, the two volumes 'The Place-Names of Western Gwent' (1991) and 'The Place-Names of Eastern Gwent' (1988) were written. Other papers have been published in the 'Gwent Local History Journal'.

The volume 'The Place-Names of Eastern Gwent' is dedicated to Sylvia, Graham Osborne's wife. She was fully involved in much of this work and her assistance in typing manuscripts was invaluable. Her unexpected death on 26th April, 1994 was a grievous blow to her husband and to her many friends.

Introduction

Gwent abounds in Welsh place-names and local interest in their interpretation is considerable and growing. But the literature on this topic is very limited. Some of the major names appear in 'Enwau Lleoedd' by Sir Ifor Williams published in 1945, in 'The Names of Towns and Cities in Britain' by M. Gelling, W.H.F. Nicolaisen and M. Richards published in 1970 or in the later 'Dictionary of Place-Names in the British Isles' by Adrian Room published in 1988. The booklet 'Welsh Place Names' by Dewi Davies lists some of the place-names in Gwent and then, very briefly, suggests meanings. Bradney in his 'History of Monmouthshire' also gives information about place-names in Gwent. The names of parishes in Gwent are discussed in two papers in the Monmouthshire Review but the only publication dealing specifically with Gwent place-names is Canon E.T. Davies' little booklet 'The Place Names of Gwent' though this is now out of print; it also requires considerable amendment.

In 1924 the author 'Shon' (C.J. Evans) compiled quite a comprehensive list of place-names of Gwent and their meanings in a dissertation submitted to the National Eisteddfod at Pontypool. The dissertation has not been published although photostat copies of the written manuscript are available in the Gwent County Records Office and in Newport Library. But this work now requires very considerable revision.

There is thus room for the present book which is meant to be a compact handbook for general readers, including readers unfamiliar with the precise geography of the region. The procedure used has followed that employed in modern place-name studies in that attempts have been made to find the earliest possible name-forms and then these have been interpreted. It has been deemed unnecessary, in a book of this sort, to give all of the considerable number of name forms now known.

The Origin of the name 'Gwent'

In C6 the territory between the rivers Usk and Wye became known as the Kingdom of Gwent. It is now clear that this name 'Gwent' originated in the following way.

The early rulers of Gwent had inherited from the Romans the city of Caerwent which became for a time their royal capital. The Roman name of this city was Venta Silurum i.e. 'market-place of the Silures'[1] (the Silures being the Celtic inhabitants of south-east Wales). When taken into the Welsh (or British) tongue, *venta* becomes prefixed by 'g' to give *guenta*; the C6 name of the royal city being Cair Guent (according to Nennius). The name of the kingdom, Guent (or Gwent) was thus taken from that of its C6 capital city. The Celtic name of Winchester, the Venta Belgarum of the Romans was also Guenta. But following the displacement of the Celts by the Saxons, the name was changed to one from OE *win* (from venta) and OE *ceastor* (chester), i.e. Winchester (this is the OE equivalent of the W Caerwent i.e. 'fortress Venta').

Wentloog (Gwynllwg)

From C6 until the Norman invasion at the end of C11 the Kingdom of Gwent was sometimes ruled separately and sometimes as part of the larger Kingdom known first as Glywysing then as Morgannwg, which extended, at times, from the Towy to the Wye. However, the territory between the mouths of the rivers Usk and Rhymney (extending to the heads of the Rhymney and the Ebbw Fawr inland) was always a component part (a cantref) of the larger kingdom. It was known as Gwynllwg (Gwynllyw and W territorial suffix 'wg') after its reputed founder Gwynllyw (also known as St. Woolos), son of Glywys, first ruler of Glywysing. Gwynllwg was one of the seven cantrefi of Glywysing (cantref from W *cant* 'hundred' and W *tref* 'estate or farm').

At some time, possibly not long before the Norman invasion, these cantrefi were, for administrative convenience, divided into smaller units called commotes (W *cymydau*). Gwynllwg was divided into two commotes. The coastlands now known as the Wentloog Levels and the low hills behind, formed one commote the name of which is not known. The uplands, from about Risca northwards, formed the second commote which became known as the Commote of Machen. The court or administrative centre of this commote may have been originally at Henllys (from W *hen* 'old' and W *llys* 'court' i.e. [the] old court') but, if so, was then moved to Lower Machen.

At the end of C11 the Normans invaded and rapidly subjugated most of south Wales. But their main interest was in the more fertile and more easily controlled lowlands where manorial systems were soon set up. The Welsh in the upland commotes such as Machen were expected to pay tribute but were left, with their native rulers, relatively undisturbed. However, in 1270 Gilbert de Clare, ruler of what was now the medieval Lordship of Glamorgan took over the upland territories and established direct rule. Gwynllwg was then run as a Marcher Lordship, at first in association with Glamorgan, then separately when the de Clare inheritance was divided after 1314. The Lordship was now known variously as the Lordship of Wentloog and the Lordship of Newport (Newport being the administrative centre).

The Lordship passed to the Staffords and then, in 1521, to the Crown. In 1536 the county of Monmouthshire, was formed by combining the old kingdom of Gwent (now divided into Marcher Lordships) with the old cantref of Gwynllwg (now the Lordship of Wentloog). One of the seven Hundreds of the new county was the Hundred of Wentloog; this, in fact, comprised much of the territory of the old cantref of Gwynllwg. The name Wentloog appears to have arisen from Gwynllwg in an attempt to link this name with that of Gwent.

PLACE NAMES
OF
WESTERN GWENT

Note on Place Names beginning with Aber

The W. *aber* means 'mouth of river or stream'. It is found in the names of places which are either:

(a) at the confluence of a river and a tributary (when the name of the place is taken from the tributary) or

(b) at the place where the river runs into the sea (when the name is taken from the river).

The names in brackets below are the Welsh forms given in 'Rhestr o Enwau Lleoedd' [266]

Aberbeeg (Aber-big)

Aberbyg (1659)[2], *Aberbyg bridge* (1709)[3]. *Aberbeeg* (1790)[4], *Nant Bige* (1577)[270], *Aber-Beeg* (1779)[271]

Village at confluence of Ebbw Fawr and Ebbw Fach, once site of 'packhorse' bridge. Once also railway junction and brewery site.

Name from W *aber* and *Big*, name of brook flowing into the Ebbw Fawr approximately 1/2 mile above the confluence. (The *Big* brook once formed the boundary between the Lordship of Abergavenny and the manor of Bryngwyn and Wentsland.)

Abercarn (Aber-carn)

uillam treficarn pont (c 942)[5], *Habercarne* (1535)[6], *Abercarne* (1690[7], 1828[8]), *Abercarn* (1829)[9], *Abercarne* (1591)[272], *Abercarn* (1659)[273]

Town at confluence of Ebbw with the Gwyddon brook, hence earlier (C 19) name Abergwyddon[10, 11]. But the first settlement in the area appears to have been farther down the valley, near the confluence of the Ebbw with the Carn brook (now Cwmcarn). The name Abercarn, appropriate to this site, appears subsequently to have been transferred to the early ironworks[1, 2] and then to the industrial village once with collieries, chemical and tinplate works which grew up approximately one mile to the north.

There are early monastic associations as indicated by local place-names e.g. Chapel Farm and Pont Mynachlog, and Abercarn 'within the Lordship of Maghen' was a manor of Llantarnam Abbey. After the dissolution of the monasteries in 1535 much of the land of this manor comprised the Lordship of Abercarn(e).

Name from W *aber* and *Carn*, name of stream.

Abersychan

Pont Abersychan (1633)[268], *Abersychan* (1836)[13], *Abersechan* (1614-15)[274], *Abersychan* (1634)[275].

Once 'waste' land in the manor of Bryngwyn and Wentsland, the name was taken from that of a farmhouse (which subsequently became the 'Fox and Hounds' inn). An ironworks (i.e. the 'British Ironworks') was established about 1830 and a large industrial village grew up, i.e. in the vicinity of the confluence of the Afon Lwyd with the Sychan brook.

Name from W *aber* and *Sychan*, name of stream.

10

Abertillery (Abertyleri, Aberteleri)

Teleri (1332)[14], *Aber-Tileri* (1779)[14, 15], *Glenteler* (1256-7)[276], *Abertillery* (1754)[277].

Industrial village, once with collieries and tinplate works situated in the valley of the Ebbw Fach near the confluence with the Tillery (Tyleri or Teleri) brook.

Name from W *aber* and *Tillery* (etc.) name of stream.

Abertysswg (Abertyswg)

Aber Towssogge (1583)[16], *Tyr Abertisuge* (1605-6)[278], *Abertusswg* (1755)[279].

Village in Rhymney valley, on western boundary of Gwent. Name originally that of farmhouse, then that of village built by the Tredegar Iron & Steel Company for workers at the McLaren Colliery (sunk in 1897) on land belonging to the farm.

Name from W *aber* and *Tysswg (Tyswg)* name of stream running into the Rhymney river at this point.

Aberystruth (Aberystrwyth)

Aberstrewyth (1391)[17], *Aberustuth* (1558[17],1577[18]), *Aberystwyth* (1533-8)[19], *Aberystwith* or *Blaenau Ghwent* (c1790)[4], *Aberystrwyth blaeney gwent* (1566)[280], *Aberystwith* which is likewise called *Blaenau Gwent* (1801)[281].

Once name of large parish also known as Blaenau Gwent (in which the industrial town of Blaina has grown up).

It is recorded that in 1779 *Koome yr ystrwyth* was also known as *Koome Kelin (Cwm Celyn)*. When parishes were formed hereabouts, this parish became *Plwyf Blaen Gwent* and *Plwyf y Blaen* (from W *plwyf* 'parish' and W *blaen* 'uplands'); hence the name *Blaina*. *Ystrwyth* may be a form of a personal name.

Name from W *aber* and *Ystrwyth*, name of brook running into the Ebbw Fach (near Blaina); the name of the little valley was later changed to *Cwm Celyn*.

Alltyryn (Allt-yr-Ynn)

Alte yr Inne (1571)[20], *Allt yr ynn* (1633)[21], *Allterin* or *Alter y yn* (1663)[22].

Originally the name of a farmhouse, now a suburb of Newport. Name from W *allt* 'cliff, steep hillside' or in S. Wales 'wooded slope' and W *ynn* = *onn* (plural of W *onnen*) 'ash tree' i.e. 'the steep slope with the ash trees'.

Argoed

Argoyd Serowy (1455)[23], *Teere argod* (Tir Argoed) (1569)[24], 1572[25]), *Argoed* (1832)[26], *Argoed Colliery* (1845)[27].

Name of a farm, later of three farms (Argoed Fawr, Ganol and Fach), then of a mining village in the Sirhowy valley north of Blackwood

Name from W *ar* 'on, upon or over' and W *coed* = *goed* 'trees or wood' giving W *argoed* 'edge of the forest or wood'[28].

Bassaleg (Basaleg)

Bassalec (c1072[29], 1101-1117[30]), *Bassaleg* (C12)[31], *Bassaleke* (1295)[32], *Bassalek* (1314)[33], *Baselick* (1609)[34], *Bassaleg* (1756)[35].

Village to the west of Newport with church on historic site; probably mother church of several churches and chapels in Gwynllwg in pre-Norman times.

The origin of this name has been the subject of controversy[36, 37]. Bassaleg is said to have been derived from W *Maes Aleg* (from *Maes Allectus* 'the field of Allectus or Aleg') supposedly being the site of a battle between Allectus and the Britons in 287 AD (according to Nennius). But the forms of the name suggest a derivation from the L. (and Greek!) *basilica* 'church or monastery' by loss of the terminal *'a'*.

Similar name-forms are found in Ireland, e.g. *Baislec;* and in Scotland (Gaelic) *Paislig* has become Paisley.

Beaufort (Cendl)

Beaufort (1792)[38], *Beaufort Works* (1807)[39], *Beaufort Iron Works* (1797)[283].

Village just north of Ebbw Vale. A blast furnace was built here in 1779 on land leased to Kendall & Co, the ironmasters, by the Duke of Beaufort[40]. Beaufort ironworks was first known locally as Cendl (W form of Kendall).

Bedwellty (Bedewelte)

Bod Mellte[41], *Bodwellte* (1441)[42], *Bedewellty* (1431)[43], *Bydwelthye* (1577)[44], *Bedweltey* (1763)[45], *Bedwellte* (1437)[284], *Bedwelti* (1494)[285], *Bodwellty* (1506)[286], *Sanan bod Mellte* (1566)[280].

Church and hamlet, site of one of the older settlements in West Gwent, on Mynydd Bedwellty, above Blackwood; the parish once being very large. Bedwellty Colliery (now closed) was sunk in the valley below in 1857.

It seems to be agreed[42] that in early name-forms the first element was W *bod* 'abode' (the form *Bodvelty* was still in use in 1778[46]). The second element appears to be the personal name *Mellte* i.e. 'Mellte's abode'. However, name forms such as *Bedwellte, Bedwelti* (above) appear to be as old as the *'bod'* forms. These

13

The Parish Church of Bedwellty which stands as one of the oldest churches in south Wales; the nave and south wall may date back to the thirteenth century. Built in typical early English style it consists of a chancel, nave north aisle, south porch and an embattled western tower which was added during some fourteenth-century extensions. The visitor or worshipper will also find some most interesting internal features such as a quite superb vestment chest of fifteenth century origin and a little walk amongst the numerous ancient gravestones will reveal the headstone of a dear lady who died in the year 1859 at the age of 110 years!

forms may have arisen by vowel interchange from an earlier precursor (now lost). But if not, they suggest an origin from W *bedw* 'birch trees' and W *elltyd* (pl. of '*allt*' 'hills or slopes') ie. 'the hills or slopes covered with birch trees'. There are still many birch trees in the area.

Bettws (Betws) nr. Newport

Bettus (1569[47], 1570[48]), *Bettus Chapel* (1577)[44], *Bettws* (1583)[49], *Bettus* (1476)[287], *henllis Bettus* (1707)[288].

Now a modern housing estate near Malpas but, not long ago, a quiet rural area with a small chapel dedicated to St. David. Name from W *betws* 'oratory or chapel' possible borrowing from OE *bede hus* 'bead house'. W *betws* may also mean 'birch grove' and this may be important where there are no ecclesiastical associations.

The name is found elsewhere in Gwent; places with this name having apparently been erected at intervals along pilgrim ways to principal abbeys.

Blackwood (Coed-duon)

Black Wood (1831)[50], *Coed dduon* (1836)[13].

Town in the Sirhowy valley which has grown up around the site of a 'model' settlement established in the early 1820s by J.H. Moggridge, an English landed gentleman and social reformer who was concerned to improve housing conditions for workers[51]. For a very short time the new settlement appears to have been known as *Tremoggridge* 'Moggridge's town' but soon took the name Blackwood, this being the English translation of the name of a nearby wood Coed Duon from W *coed* 'wood' and *duon* from W *du* 'black or dark' i.e. 'dark wood'.

The W name is found elsewhere in Gwent e.g. Coed duon nr. Usk.

At the head of the river Afon Lwyd lies the town of Blaenavon which achieved World Heritage Status in the year 2001 thanks to a rich industrial past of international importance. Seen here are perhaps the finest surviving examples of eighteenth-century blast furnaces anywhere and are a permanent monument to the early steelmakers of the area, attracting many visitors from the world over.

Blaenavon (Blaenafon)

Blaen Avon (1531)[52], *Blaenafon* (1748)[53], *Blaen-Afon* (1792)[54], *Blaen-Afon Furnace* (1806)[55].

An early iron (then steel) manufacturing town, the setting for Alexander Cordell's novel 'Rape of the Fair Country'. Iron ore was first mined here for forges at Pontypool (in C15). Small-scale smelting commenced here in 1600 and the first blast furnace was in operation in 1789 (the first coal mines were opened, for coke production, in 1782).

Steel was made here from phosphate-containing iron ores in 1877-80 in experimental work by Sydney Gilchrist Thomas and Percy Gilchrist. The remains of some late C18 blast furnaces have been preserved and Big Pit Colliery, nearby, is now open as a working museum.

The town stands at the headwaters of the Afon Lwyd (known in C16 simply as Afon): the first reference to the name being to 'a brook called Blaen Avon'. The name is from W *blaen* 'top, end or tip' and W *afon* 'river' but in this case also the name of the river i.e. 'head of the (river) Afon'.

Blaina (Blaenau)

Blanagwent (1577)[44], *Blayne Gwent* (1594)[56], *Blaenau Gwent* (1700)[56], *Aberystwith* or *Blaenau Ghwent* (1790)[4].

Small industrial town in the valley of the Ebbw Fach north of Abertillery which has grown out of the old parish of Aberystruth or Blaenau Gwent. Blaina was formerly associated with iron manufacture and coal mining.

The name Blaina has come from Blaenau Gwent, the second element having been lost and the terminal *'au'* of the first has become *'a';* this may reflect the Gwentian pronunciation of the name which is from W *blaen* 'top, end or tip' pl. *blaenau* 'uplands', so Blaenau Gwent is 'uplands of Gwent'. Blaenau Gwent is also the name of the modern borough at the heads of the Ebbw and Sirhowy valleys.

British

Site of former ironworks (1830-1876) on hill above Abersychan. Name from that of works 'British Ironworks' (Small, Shears & Taylor).

Bryn Awel

Name of estate of post World War I houses on hill above Wattsville. Name from W *bryn* 'hill' and W *awel* 'wind, breeze' i.e. 'windy hill'.

Brynmawr (Bryn-mawr)

Bryn-mawr (1832)[57], *Gwain yr Helycen* (1790-8)[289], *Bryn Mawr* (1813)[290], *Bryn Mawr farm* (1816-49)[291].

Built on moorlands to the south of the Brecon Beacons, Brynmawr is situated at one of the highest altitudes of any town in Wales. The name of the site was originally Gwaun Helygen from W *gwaun* 'moorland or mountain pasture' and W *helygen* 'willow tree i.e. 'the willow tree on the moorland'. But when a town grew up in this locality towards the middle of C19 the above name was superseded by Brynmawr which was chosen as the name of the ecclesiastical parish which was then formed.

Name from W *bryn* 'hill or mountain' and W *mawr* 'big, large or great' i.e. 'the big hill or mountain'.

18

Exciting excavations resulting in important Roman 'finds' were conducted at Caerleon's amphitheatre during the 1920s as this scene depicts and the doyen of such an operation - Sir Mortimer Wheeler led the undertaking.

Caerleon

An ancient town on the Usk, near Newport. In Roman times it was Headquarters of the Second Augustan Legion. There are many Roman remains including an amphitheatre, bath-buildings, the foundations of barrack blocks and a stretch of Roman wall. Many interesting relics are housed in a museum.

Early name-forms are *Iscae Leg II Augusta, Isca,* (early 3rd century), *Isca Augusta* (late 7th century), *urbe leogis quae brittanicae Cair Lion dicitus* (944)[292] (ie. 'The city of the legions which the British call *'Cair Lion'*), *Carleoin, Carlion* (1086)[293], *Kaerlegion* (c1130-1144)[294], *Karlion* (c1291)[295], *Gaerlleon, Caerllion* (c1450)[296].

The name has been derived from OW *Cair*, W *caer* 'fort' and L *legion*(is) i.e. 'fort of the Legion'.[58]

Castell-y-bwch

Castle y bwche (1690)[59], *Castle buch* (1690)[60], *Castell-y-bwch* (1707)[61].

Hamlet near Henllys with inn of same name. The name has been derived from W *castell* 'castle' and W *bwch* 'buck' suggested as a 'mocking' name for a deserted, ruined place[62].

Castleton (Cas-bach)

Casbach (1536-9)[63], *Castle Town* (1787)[11], *Castle Farm* or *Castleton* (1814)[65], *Litell Castell* (1447-8)[297], *Casteletonne* (1595)[298], *Castletowne* (1687)[299].

Village between Newport and Cardiff, once site of (Wentloog) castle, hence the name Castletown i.e. 'settlement by a castle'. The W *Casbach* means 'little castle'.

Cefn, Rogerstone

Keven tyr marchog (1595)[66], *Keven Tyre Marchog* (1625)[67].

Ridge near Rogerstone along which one of the main roads from the Western Valleys to Newport passes (via Highcross). Original name from W *cefn* 'ridge' W *tir* 'land' and W *marchog* 'knight or horseman' i.e. 'the ridge on the knight's land'.

Sir Hywel Lord of Caerleon's son 'Syr Morgan' is said to have been killed on Cefn tir-y-Marchog in C13[68].

Cefn Fforest

Cefn-y-Fforest (1840)[69].

Originally name of a farmhouse on a ridge to the north of Blackwood, then of a village which grew up nearby. Name from W *cefn* 'ridge' and W *fforest* 'forest' but, more often 'parkland or open country' i.e. 'the ridge in the 'fforest''

Cefn Golau

Part of Tredegar, houses on lower slopes of Mynydd Bedwellty. A derivation from W *cefn* 'ridge' and W *golau* 'light' has been proposed but 'ridge of light' seems not to be very meaningful.

The W *olau* (pl. of *ol*) 'trackway' particularly 'ancient trackway'[70] may have been confused here with W [g]olau 'light', an extraneous 'g' having been added. Derivation from W *olau* would then give 'ridge of the ancient trackway'. An ancient trackway Sarn hir (W *sarn* 'causeway' and W *hir* 'long' i.e. '[the] long causeway') did indeed run along Cefn Golau from Bedwellty, proceeding over Mynydd Llangynidr to Crickhowell and Brecon.

Cefn Mably (Cefn Mabli)

Kevenmably (1618)[267].

Once a mansion; home of the Kemeys family from C16 to C18, then for some years a hospital; about 6 miles north-east of Cardiff, on Gwent border. Name from W *cefn* 'ridge' and W *Mabli* 'Mabel' i.e. 'Mabel's ridge'[71]. This Mabel was probably the heiress of Robert Fitzhamon the Norman conqueror of Glamorgan at the end of C11.

Celynnen, Newbridge

Kelynan farmhouse (1707)[72].

This farmhouse appears to have taken its name from a brook once known as Celynen which flows through the little valley known as Cwm Hafod Fach. The name subsequently became that of a part of Newbridge and of the two Newbridge collieries (both now closed), North Celynen and South Celynen, respectively.

Name from W *celynnen* 'holly tree'.

Coedkernew (Coedcernyw)

Cockneu (1295)[32], *Coyckernue* (1314)[33], *Coyd Kernewe* (1568)[73], *Coydkirne* (1577)[44], *Coed Kernew* (1778)[74], *Coittarnen* (c1102)[300], *Koytherneu* (1230-40)[301], *Coitarneu, Koytherneu* (1350)[302].

Village on Wentloog Levels, between Newport and Cardiff. Name from W *coed* 'wood or trees' and the personal name *Cernyw* (reputed son of Gwynllyw) i.e. 'Cernyw's wood'.

The name Cernyw usually has Cornish rather than Welsh associations, being, indeed the Welsh name for Cornwall.

Coed-y-paen (Coed-y-paun)

Coed mab Payn (1558)[75], *Coed map paen* (1647)[303], *Coed-y-pain* (1729)[304].

Hamlet in the parish of Llangibby near 'Llandegfedd' Reservoir. Name from W *coed* 'trees or wood' and *Paun* from the family name Payne (not from W *paun* peacock) i.e. 'Paynes' Wood.

Crindau (Crindai) Newport

Crindye (1577)[44], *the Crindye* (1607)[76], *the Crindey* (1651)[77], *Crindau Farm* (1792)[78], *Crinde* (1427)[305], *Crindau* (1568-80)[306].

Part of Newport, once site of an Elizabethan manor house (Crindau House), an old Herbert residence; the porch still stands. Probable derivation from W *crindy* 'thatched house'[64].

Croesllanfro, Rogerstone

Croes Willym Bro (1621)[79], *Croes Gwillim Bro* (1662)[80], *Croes Wyllim bro* (1601)[307], *Cross William Bro ffarm* (1814)[308].

Originally name of farmhouse near crossroads (adjoining Mescoed Mawr) above Rogerstone. The name Croes Gwilym Bro was in use in the 1850s; this name from W *croes* 'crossroads or cross' W *Gwilym* 'William' and W *bro = fro* 'vale' i.e. 'the crossroads of William's vale' (c.f. Tregwilym!).

The name appears to have been changed to Croeslanfro, from W *glan = lan* 'bank or rising land' and then, as often happens, W *lan* has become *llan* 'church' giving Croesllanfro the crossroads of the church in the vale'. This is topographically incorrect since the only church in the district, that at Henllys, is some distance away.

Croespenmaen

Crosspenmay (1787)[11], *Cross Pen Main* (c1790)[4], *le crosse pen Maine* (1627)[309], *cros pen maine* (1690-1)[210].

Hamlet with C18 Tithe Barn, then mining village between Oakdale and Crumlin; near crossroads on old road to Penmaen. Name from W *croes* 'crossroads or cross' and Penmaen.

Croesyceiliog

Gwayne Croes y Kyloge (1653)[81], *Cross y Ceilog* (c1790)[4].

Near Cwmbran, Gwent Council Offices and Gwent Police Headquarters are here. Name from W *croes* 'crossroads or cross' and W *ceiliog* 'cock', the latter apparently referring to the sign of an ancient inn on the road to Panteg[82]. The name is also found in Llandyfaelog parish in Dyfed.

Crosskeys

Kemere (1447-8)[313], *pont y Cymmer* (1695)[314], *Pontycymmer* (1836)[315].

Industrial village near the confluence of the Ebbw and Sirhowy rivers although the name was first used for houses built to the north of the 'Crosskeys' inn during the latter half of C19. Newtown, near the above confluence, now part of Crosskeys was formerly in North Risca.

The name has been taken from that of the inn. There is no connection with the former dedication of the church in nearby Risca to St. Peter (sign of the crossed keys); the dedication was changed in 1773 (to St. Michael) long before Crosskeys was built (the dedication was changed again, to St. Mary, in 1856 when a new church was built).

The hidden confluence. The meeting place of the rivers Sirhowy (left) and Ebbw (right) at Crosskeys. (by courtesy of Mr. Derek John).

25

The bridge over the Ebbw, formerly in Mynyddislwyn parish was once known as Pont-y-cymmer[83, 84] (from W *pont* 'bridge' and W *cymer* 'confluence' i.e. 'bridge of the confluence').

Garnant (near Ammanford) in W. Wales was once known as Crosskeys as, until 1950, were the houses near Walnut Tree Viaduct, Nantgarw. In both cases the name was taken from that of an inn.

Crumlin (Crymlyn)

Grimlin (1630)[85], *Pont Grymlyn* (1710)[86], *Pont Crwmlyn* (1787)[11], *Crumlin Bridge* (1807)[87].

Village north of Newbridge in Ebbw valley; name formerly that of a farmhouse and of a bridge across the Ebbw. It is situated below a pronounced bend in the Ebbw Valley, hence the name Crymlyn from W *crymu* 'to bend' and W *glyn* 'valley'[88] i.e. 'the bend in the valley' or 'the crooked valley'. Crumlin was once the site of a massive railway viaduct across the Ebbw Valley (built 1857, and closed for use in 1964).

The name is found elsewhere in Wales, e.g. Crymlyn near Margam, also in Northern Ireland (Crumlin, Antrim).

Note on Place-names commencing with Cwm.

There are several Welsh words meaning 'valley' i.e. *cwm, glyn, dyffryn* and *pant*. The first one *cwm* derived from a Celtic word for 'trough' is used to describe the steep-sided 'end' valleys so often found in South Wales. In place-names *cwm* is generally followed by the name of the river or stream flowing down the valley; this is then the name of the valley itself.

The town of Crumlin as it appeared during the 1950s with its majestic viaduct, a feat of Victorian engineering that carried railway traffic safely across the Ebbw valley for more than a hundred years.

Cwm near Ebbw Vale

Cwmmerddych (1857)[89], *Cwm Merddog*[69], *Koom Mythve* (1779)[316], *Cwm Mythwe* (1801)[317], *Abermurthyach* (1807)[318].

Colliery village (Marine Colliery now closed) in the valley of the Ebbw Fawr south of Ebbw Vale, near the confluence with the brook named Merddog on the current 1" OS map. On earlier maps the name is given as Abermurthyach[90] and Abermythve[91] also appears to have been used.

The present name is from W *cwm* 'valley' and *Merddog*, name of brook; this second element has now been lost, but may originally have been *Myrdd fach*[386, 387].

Cwmavon (Cwmafon)

Cwm Avon (1314)[33], *Cwm Avon Mill* (1836)[13], *Cwmb Avon* (1771)[319].

Small village in the upper reaches of the Afon Lwyd, below Blaenavon, once with ironworks. A row of early ironworkers' cottages here has been restored.

The name has been taken from that of the valley, i.e. from W *cwm* 'valley' and *Afon*, old name of Afon Lwyd, 'valley of the Afon'.

Cwmbran

Bran (1314)[33], *Cwmbran* (1707)[92], *Cwmbrane* (1764, 1803)[92], *Nant brane* (1452)[320], *Nant y Braen* (1698)[321], *Cwmbran* (1810)[322].

Town at the confluence of the brook Bran with the Afon Lwyd. An industrial town with collieries, chemical works, iron and tinworks grew up here during the latter half of C19 and later. Cwmbran was designated a New Town in 1949 and has accordingly increased in size.

This is probably the original road bridge that crossed the Afon Lwyd at Cwmavon, the scene having been photographed in about 1900. In the background is Forge Row; the group of twelve cottages that were constructed in 1805 for workers at the nearby Varteg forge and fully restored as privately occupied listed buildings in recent years.

The name is from W *cwm* 'valley' and *Bran*, name of stream flowing down from Upper Cwmbran; the town has taken its name from this little valley.

Cwmcarn (Cwm-carn)

Cwincarn (1830)[93], *Cwmcarn* (1833)[94].

Village south of Abercarn near the confluence of the *Carn* brook with the river Ebbw. Once Abercarn, but when this name was taken by the industrial village which grew up to the north, the village which developed here became Cwmcarn (originally the name of the *Carn* valley). Name from W *cwm* 'valley' and *Carn*, name of brook.

Cwmfelinfach (Cwmfelin-fach)

Felin Fach (1839)[90], *Cwm felin fach* (1836)[13].

Village originally built 1900-1910 for workers at nearby Nine Mile Point Colliery. There was once a corn mill here on the banks of Nant Draenog. Babell (W *pabell* 'tent or tabernacle') Calvinistic Methodist Chapel dates from 1823 (now a memorial to the poet Islwyn).

The name is from W *cwm* 'valley', W *melin = felin* 'corn mill' and W *bach = fach* 'small' i.e. 'the valley with the small corn mill'.

Cwmtillery (Cwmtyleri)

Cwm Tilery (c1790)[4].

Small colliery village above Abertillery near the confluence of the Ebbw Fach and the Tillery (Tyleri) brook. Name from W *cwm* 'valley' and *Tillery*, name of brook; this was originally the name of the little valley itself.

Cwmynyscoy

Industrial village near Pontypool. Name from W *cwm* 'valley' W *ynys* 'island or water-meadow' and W *gau* 'hollow' i.e. 'the valley with the water-meadow in the hollow'.

The names Ynys Gau[95] and Ynys goi[96] are found in Glamorgan.

Danygraig (Dan-y-Graig) Risca

Part of Risca, near the New Cemetery, at the foot of the rocky slope known as 'The Graig'. Name from W *tan* = *dan* 'below' and W *craig* 'rock, crag or cliff' but here also actual name i.e. 'below the Graig' or 'below the rocky slope'.

Duffryn (Dyffryn) Newport

Deffren Ebboth (1295)[32], *Diffrin* (1669)[97], *Diffryn, Dyffryn* (1447-8)[326].

Once a manor, now part of Newport near the mouth of the River Ebbw. From W *dyffryn* 'valley' (in sense of 'through' valley rather than 'end' valley). Name found frequently elsewhere in Gwent.

Dukestown near Tredegar

Name given to houses built on land belonging to the Duke of Beaufort during the period of industrial expansion in the area.

Ebbw Vale (Glynebwy)

Glyn Eboth (1317)[98], *Eboth* (1101-20)[327], *Eboth* (1146-7)[328], *Glyneboth* (1476)[329], *Pen-y-cae* (1757)[330], *Ebwy Vale Furnace* (1790)[331], *Ebbw Vale* (1791)[332], *Penycae Ebbw Vale* (1802)[333].

Town at the head of the valley of the Ebbw Fawr. The first iron furnaces were built here in 1787 on land at Pen-y-cae farm. Ironworks, steelworks and collieries developed. A giant steelworks 2¹/₂ miles long was opened in 1936 but is scheduled for complete closure in 2002. Site of 1992 Garden Festival.

The name is from the English equivalent of W *glyn* 'valley or vale' and *Ebbw (Ebwy)* name of river.

Fleur de Lis

Flower de Luce (1846)[99].

Village near Pengam and site (along the line of the old Rumney tramroad) of a 'model' settlement established by J.H. Moggridge in the 1820s (see Blackwood).

The first name appears to have been Trelyn, this being the name of a nearby farmhouse, but it then became *Fleur de lis* from Fr. *fleur* 'flower' and Fr. *lis* 'lily' i.e. 'lily flower', the old French imperial symbol.

The name was originally that of a public house (c1831[334]) which was in this vicinity at the time the settlement was established.

Garnddyrys

Site near Blaenavon; associations with Alexander Cordell's 'Rape of the Fair Country'. An ironworks was erected here by Hill & Hopkins in 1800. Pig iron and iron bars were manufactured and a rolling mill erected. But in 1860 activity was transferred to Blaenavon and the site has since been empty.

Name from W *carn* = *garn* (lost definite article) 'cairn, pile of stones or, more possibly 'hill' and W *dyrys* = *ddyrys* 'difficult, tangled' i.e. 'the hillside which is difficult to negotiate'.

Garndiffaith

Garney diffoth (1664)[269], *Garn defrith* (1836)[13], *Karnediffeth* (1590)[335], *Garn diffeth* (1699)[336].

Industrial village north of Pontypool, name from W *carn = garn* (sign of missing definite article i.e. *y garn*) 'cairn, pile of stones' but also 'hill or mountain' and W *diffaith* 'waste or desert'. The name has been interpreted as 'wilderness cairn' but the most probable meaning is 'the barren hill' or 'wilderness hill'.

Gelligroes (Gelli-groes)

Kelly grose (1538-44)[100], *Gellygroes* (1833)[101].

Small village in Sirhowy valley south of Pontllanfraith. A water-powered corn mill was in use here until quite recently.

The name is from W *celli = gelli* 'grove of trees' and W *croes = groes* 'crossroads or cross i.e. 'the grove at the crossroads' or possibly 'the grove with the cross'.

Gilwern

Gilwern (1810-16)[337].

Village 2 miles west of Abergavenny at south end of Brecon Canal (centre for canal boat hire). Name from W *cil = gil* 'retreat' and W *gwern = wern* alder trees' i.e. 'the retreat in the alder trees'; ('retreat' here probably means a hermit's residence).

Glascoed

Glascoyd (1537)[102], *Glascoide* (1578)[103], *Glascoed* (1623)[104].

Village between Usk and Pontypool, site of Ordnance Factory, once a 'wood and waste'. Name from. W *glas* 'green [or blue]' and W *coed = goed* 'trees or wood' i.e. 'Greenwood'. In fact the name suggests a young or a coppiced wood.

The Old Mill Gelligroes with its water wheel fed by the Sirhowy river. It was here, thanks to its own electricity generating system, that radio messages were received from the ill-fated Titanic as she sank with great loss of life in April 1912. The old mill now serves as an interesting museum.

Glasllwch, Newport

le glaslough (1599-60)[105], *Glaslooche* (1607)[106], *Glasllwch Farm* (1856)[107], *Glaslowe* (1447-8)[338], *Glas lughe* (1553)[339].

Once the name of a farm, now that of a suburb of Newport. Name from W *glas* 'green [or blue]' and W *llwch*, old word synonymous with W *llyn* 'lake, pool or pond' i.e. 'the green pond or pool'.

Goytre (Goetre Fawr)

Goytre (1525)[108], *Coytre* (c1348)[340], *Goytre* (1520)[341], *Y Goytre* (c1566)[280].

Village between Pontypool and Abergavenny. Name from W *coed* = *goed* 'wood or trees' and W *tref* originally 'estate'; modern meaning 'home or town' so 'home in the woods' or 'estate in the woods'.

Golynos

Y Gelynos (1654)[109], *Gelynos ffarm* (1814)[342], *Gelynos* (Panteg)(1682)[343], *Golynos* (Panteg)(1683)[344].

Name of farm near Rogerstone with celebrated very large oak tree felled in 1810 but the names Golynos and Gelynos are found in a number of other places in Gwent e.g. Golynos near Abersychan, former ironworks site.

Gelynos appears to be the original name form, from W *celyn* = *gelyn* (after lost definite article) 'holly trees' with the diminutive ending *'os'* 'the small holly trees'.

Govilon (Gofilon)

Village near Abergavenny near present south end of Brecon Canal; Canal office of British Waterways here. Name probably from W *gefaillon* 'forges' indicating an ancient ironworking site.

Griffithstown

Coed-y-grigg ycha (1648)[345], *Coed-y-Grick* (1766)[346].

Village near Pontypool once with ironworks. Houses for railway workers were built here and the place is named after Henry Griffiths, first stationmaster at Pontypool Railway Station[110]. He initiated the Pontypool Road Benefit Building Society in 1866; this Society built houses on land previously known as Coed-y-gric.

Hafodrisclawdd (Hafod-yr-isclawdd)

Hafod yr ysclawdd (1836)[13].

Name of three farmhouses (Hafodrisclawdd Fawr, Ganol and Fach) on hillside above the Sirhowy valley, near Markham; also of early colliery. Name from W *hafod* 'summer dwelling' and W *isclawdd* 'the lower dyke or embankment' i.e. 'the summer dwelling near the lower dyke or embankment'.

Under the old Welsh system of farming (transhumance), cattle were moved up into the hills to graze during the summer months and a temporary summer dwelling *(hafod)* was erected.

Embankments or dykes were boundary markers. An embankment runs across Cefn Manmoel some 4 miles to the north of Hafodrisclawdd; this presumably was the 'upper' embankment.

Hafodyrynys

Hafod Yrynys (1534)[111], *Hafod ar enys* (1540-1)[112], *Havodyrinis* (1582)[113]

Name of farmhouse then, later, a village near Crumlin on top of a steep hill (Hafodyrynys hill). There is here a stream on which there was once a Cistercian corn mill.

Name from W *hafod* 'summer dwelling' (see Hafodrisclawdd) and W *ynys* 'island or river meadow' obviously the latter in this case, i.e. 'the summer dwelling near the water meadow'.

Henllys

Henthles (123040)[114], *Henllis* (1542-3)[115], *Henllis* (1651)[116], *Hentllys* (1769)[117].

Once, fairly recently, a small village with a church on an ancient site in the countryside west of Cwmbran but locality now much developed. Henllys may have been the site of the *llys* 'court' of the ruler of the pre-Norman Commote of Machen (i.e. the upland portion of the Cantref of Gwynllwg) prior to its removal to Machen, hence the name from W *hen* 'old' and W *llys* 'court' i.e. '[the] old court'.

Note the presence of an intrusive 't' in the name-forms, this being an attempt to represent the pronunciation of the W '*ll*' after '*hen*'.

The name is found elsewhere in Gwent (Henllys near Tregare) and in Wales.

Hollybush

Former mining village in the Sirhowy valley north of Argoed. There was a colliery here in the 1820s but major mining operations commenced in the 1880s when many families moved into the area. The name was taken from that of the inn. It is found elsewhere in Gwent (e.g. Cwmbran).

Note on Place-names commencing with 'Llan'.

In modern Welsh *llan* means 'church' but the original meaning was 'enclosure'.

The 6th century in Wales was a time of great missionary activity by the Celtic church. Missionary preachers would travel from place to place, often along the line of Roman roads, preaching wherever they could find congregations. In places where they were successful a little mud and wattle 'church' would be built, with other huts, in an enclosure (the llan) which came to take the name of a missionary 'saint'.

The churches which, over the years, survived were subsequently rebuilt in more permanent materials but continued to bear the llan name and the name of the 'saint' to which the church was dedicated. Later on some dedications were changed, often to better-known saints.

Llanbadoc (Llanbadog Fawr)

Llanmadock (1254)[118], *Lampadoc* (1295)[32], *Llanbadock* (1538-44)[119], *Lambadoch* (1577)[44].

Village near Usk with church (from which it has taken its name) once belonging to the Benedictine nuns of Usk Priory. The name is from W *llan* 'church' and the 'saint's' name *Madog = Badog* i.e. 'Madog's Church'.

Llanddewi Fach

Llanddeui Penn Bei (C12)[120], *Llanthewy* (1577)[44], *Llanthewi Fach* (1833)[101].

Church near Llandegveth, completely restored in 1920. Name from W *llan* 'church', W personal name *Dewi = Ddewi* 'David' and W *bach = fach* 'small or little' i.e. 'the little church of St. David'. The distinguishing adjective 'little' is necessary because there are other parishes of the same name in Wales.

Llandegveth (Llandegfedd)

Podum Merthir Tecmed (c750)[122], *Ecclesia proinde Tegceued* (c1155)[123], *Llandegeueth* (1314)[33], *Llandegueth* (1577)[44].

Village 2 miles east of Croesyceiliog which has taken its name from its church. Reputed site of the martyrdom of Tecmed (mother of Teilo) by the Saxons.

The name is from W *llan* 'church' and the personal name *Tecmed* i.e. 'Tecmed's Church'.

Llanelen

Sancta Elena (1254)[118], *Lomelens* (1583)[124], *Llanelen* (1535)[347], *Lanelen* (1586-7)[348].

Village 2 miles south of Abergavenny. Name from W *llan* 'church' and the personal name *Elen* i.e. 'Elen's Church'. Who this Elen was is not known precisely.

Llanelly (Llanelli)

Llanelly (1518-29)[125], *Llaneley* (1610)[126], *Llanelly* (1829)[13], *Lann Elthy* (1314)[349], *Llanelly* (1518-29)[350].

Church and village on hill above Gilwern; John Hanbury is said to have constructed an iron forge near here in 1680[127].

Name from W *llan* 'church' and the personal name *Elli* i.e. 'Elli's Church'. The Elli to which the church is dedicated was a disciple of St. Cadoc (Cadwg) and reputedly succeeded him as Abbot of Llancarvan.

There is, of course, a much better-known Llanelly (Llanelli) in West Wales.

Llanfair Kilgeddin (Llanfair Cilgedin)

Kilgindyn (1254)[118], *Kilgudyn* (1291)[128], *Lammer Kyheden* (1577)[44], *Llanfair Cilcydyn* (1584)[354].

Village and church (now closed but with unusual internal decorations) on the banks of the river Usk 4 miles upstream from the town of Usk.

Cilgedyn = Cilcydyn from W *cil* 'retreat' and the personal name *Cudyn* i.e. 'Cudyn's place of retreat'. Llanfair from W *llan* 'church' and the personal name *Mair* = *Fair* 'Mary', so the name is 'The church of St. Mary [at or near] Cudyn's place of retreat'.

Llanfoist (Llan-ffwyst Fawr)

Llanfoist (1254)[118], *Llanfoyst* (1577)[44], *Lanfoyst* (c1348)[351].

Village on Brecon Canal near Abergavenny named after church (rebuilt by Crawshay Bailey in 1905). Name from W *llan* 'church' and the personal name *Ffwyst* (C6 saint from Anglesey).

Llanfrechfa

Llanhirghy (1295)[32], *Llanvrechva* (1452)[129], *Llanureghuaye* (1577)[44], *ll. frechfa* (c1566)[280].

Village and church near Llantarnam, name apparently of fairly late origin from W *llan* 'church' and W *brechfa* = *frechfa* 'spotted or speckled place'. The fields around the village display a profusion of quartz conglomerate pebbles, cobbles and even boulders of the Upper Old Red Sandstone; this is probably the origin of 'speckled place'.

The name Brechfa is found elsewhere in Wales.

The boathouse on the banks of the canal at Llanfoist, a structure that was built in about 1815 when the waterway was the vital link for the transportation of minerals to the docklands of Newport.

Llangibby (Llangybi)

ecclesia de Lancubi (1155~83)[123], *Tregrug* (1254)[118], *Llangeby* (1577)[44], *Llangibby* (1784)[131].

Village between Caerleon and Usk with Llangibby Castle (actually a mansion house) and, nearby, the site of the much older Tregrug Castle, once centre for the Lordship of Tregrug. Name from that of church i.e. from W *llan* 'church' and the personal name *Cybi* i.e. 'St Cybi's Church' Cybi was a famous Cornish saint.[132] The name *Tregrug* is from W *tre* 'estate' or 'farm' and W *grug* 'mound' ie. 'the estate on the mound'. *Tregrug Castle* is situated prominently on a low hill.

Llanhennock (Llanhynwg, Llanhenwg)

Llanhennoch (1610)[133], *Lanhenok* (1473)[353], *Llanhenocke* (1491)[354].

Hamlet near Caerleon with church on early site, Name from W *llan* 'church' and the personal name *Hynwg*[134] i.e. 'Hynwg's Church'.

Llanhilleth (Llanhiledd)

Llanhyledd (1566)[135], *Llanhylthe* (1577)[44], *Llanhilleth* (1763)[46], *Llanhyddel* (1833)[94].

Village on hill south of Aberbeeg with church (now closed) on ancient site. Name from W *llan* 'church' and the personal name *Hiledd* (reputed daughter of Cyndrwyn, C6 King of Brycheiniog[136]) i.e. 'Hiledd's Church'. The dedication of the church has been changed from Hiledd to the better-known Illtyd.

The cartographers Saxton and Speed also have a 'Llanhileth' to the south of Abergavenny. This should read 'Llanelen'.

Llanhilleth, which was once yet another centre of industry in the Ebbw Valley has experienced many changes to its landscape since this picture was taken.

Llanover (Llanofer Fawr)

Llanover (1291)[137], *Llannovore* (1353)[138], *Llanover* (1610)[139], *Lammover* (1285)[355], *Lanmovor* (1349-53)[356], *Llannover* (1535)[357].

Church and village 4 miles south of Abergavenny. In 1826 Llanover Court and the surrounding estate was purchased by Sir Benjamin Hall (later Lord Llanover).

The origin of this name has been the subject of controversy. Lady Llanover's derivation from St. Gofor is suspect.[140] A derivation from W *llan* 'church' and W personal name *Mofor* or *Myfor* has been proposed i.e. 'Myfor's Church'.

Llantarnam also Llanvihangel Llantarnam

Emsanternon (c1179)[141], *Dewma in Nant-Teyrnon,* also *Monastery of Caerleon* (1179)[142], *Lanterna* (1273)[143], *Llanternham* (1536-9)[144], *Lanterneham* (1654)[145], *Y Mynachlog Ydeyma* (C16)[146].

Now village with industrial sites adjoining Malpas near Newport. Once site of Cistercian Abbey founded by Sir Hywel ap Iorwerth, Lord of Caerleon in 1179. First founded as the Abbey of Caerleon or Dewma (site unknown) then as Emsanternon, Lanterna etc. on present site (known also as Vallium (1244) from L *valles* 'valley').

Much of the surrounding land and the mountainous land in what is now West Gwent was farmed (divided into granges) by the monks of this monastery in medieval times.

The name *Emsanternon* has been derived from Ynys Nant Teyrnon (i.e. from W *ynys* 'watermeadow', W *nant* = originally 'valley' then 'stream [running though valley]' and the W personal name *Teyrnon* (an early ruler of Gwent). W *nant* has then become W *llan* to give Llantarnam; a similar change of *nant* to *llan* has been observed elsewhere (e.g. Llancarfan).

44

The first reference to the church of St. Michael appears in 1535[147], name from W *llan* 'church' and *Mihangel = Fihangel* 'Michael' so Llanfihangel is 'Church of St. Michael'.

Llanvihangel Pontymoel (Llanfihangel Pont-y-moel)

Llannyhangel Pontemoiel (1577)[44], *Kilgoigen* (1254)[118], *Kilgoygan* (1291)[137], *Kilgoyan* (1619)[148], *Llanfihangell Pont y Moyle* (1606)[358], *Llanvihangel Kilgoygan* otherwise *Lanvihangel Pont Moel* (1636)[359].

Village near Pontypool with early church dedicated to St. Michael hence Llanfihangel from W *llan* 'church' and *Mihangel = Fihangel* 'Michael' i.e. 'St Michael's Church'.

The earliest name of the district appears to have been *Cilgoegan* from W *cil* 'retreat' and the W personal name *Coegan* (also the name of a brook)[149] suggesting the site of a hermitage.

Following the establishment of an early ironworks at nearby Pont-y-moel in C16[150], the church of St. Michael, though 1^1/$_2$ miles away, came to be identified with the village which developed near the ironworks and the name was changed to Llanvihangel Pontymoel. The second element has arisen from W *pont* 'bridge' and W *moel* 'bare' or 'bare hill' i.e. 'the bridge of the bare hill'.

Llanyrafon

Lanyrafon (1836)[13].

Now name of part of Cwmbran, built around the ancient farm and manor house near the banks of the Afon Lwyd and known previously as Lanyrafon. This name has come from W *glan = lan* 'river bank or rising ground' and W *afon* 'river' or more possibly *Afon*, name of river i.e. '[on] the banks of the Afon'. Over the years W *lan* has become confused with W *llan* 'church' and this is reflected in the present name.

Machen

Mahhayn (1101-17)[30], *Magheyn* (1230-40)[151], *Machhein* (1262)[152], *Meghen* (1295)[32], *Maghay* (1314)[33], *Maghen* (1536-9)[153], *Mauchen* (1577)[44], *Machen* (1695)[154].

The industrial village on the Rhymney river given the name Machen on the current 1" OS map is a relatively recent development, the name being originally that of a village, a mile or so to the south, now marked as Lower Machen. In Roman times lead mining was carried on here and later on it was, for a time, the centre from which the pre Norman Commote of Machen and then the Lordship of Machen was ruled.

The origin of the name Machen has been the subject of controversy. But a possible clue to a solution of the problem may be drawn from the list of name forms given. It can be seen that *'ayn'* or *'eyn'* in the older forms becomes *'en'* in later forms. These early name-forms are indeed reminiscent of those of the old cantref of Mechain in North-east Wales (where forms such as *Machain, Maghen* and *Maghan* have been noted). This name has been derived from W *ma* 'place' or 'plain' and *Cain*, the name of a river, suggested as possibly also a personal name[155].

In the Book of Llan Dav[156] there are references to *Nant Cein* and *Inis (Ynys) Cein* in the parish of Llangoven (Gwent) and there is a reference to a fishery in the Usk called the *Ceyne* (1383)[157]. It is possible that all of these names may have arisen from a personal name such as Kein (Ceinwen) one of the daughters of Brychan, King of Brycheiniog[158]. The name Machen (Machein) may have thus originated from W *ma* 'place' or 'plain' and this personal name *Kein*.

It has been pointed out that in the manuscripts of Iolo Morgannwg, Machen is described as 'Meigan Cil Ceincoed'[159]. The derivation of Machen suggested here is from the personal name Meugan (which does not fit the name forms) and Ceincoed has

Western Gwent is still a place for seeking the remains of once-important landmarks, one of which is the Victorian-built viaduct at Maesycwmmer seen here in about 1910.

been translated as 'forest' (from W *ceincio* 'to branch' and W *coed* 'trees or wood'). But the presence of the personal name Cein suggests 'Cein's wood' and supports the derivation proposed.

Maesycwmmer (Maesycymer)

Village 3 miles west of Blackwood, towards the Rhymney valley. The village name appears to have been taken from that of a house built in the locality in 1826 by Rev. John Jenkins, Minister of Hengoed Baptist Church[160]. The house name was apparently from W *maes* 'meadow' and W *cymer* 'confluence' i.e. 'the meadow at the confluence'. A small stream runs into the Rhymney hereabouts but there is no major confluence. However, the house was approached by an unusual footbridge[360] and this may be the origin of the name, ie. from W *cwmer* 'footbridge'.

Malpas, Newport

Malpas (1239)[161], *Malopassu* (1314)[33], *Y Malpas* (1566)[162], *Malpas* (1577)[44], *Malpas* (1132)[361], *Malo Passo* (1239)[362].

A north-west suburb of Newport. The old road west from Caerleon traversed difficult (wet) country hereabouts. Hence the name from Fr *mal* 'bad' and Fr *pas* 'passage' i.e. 'the bad passage'[161].

The name Malpas is found twice in England.

Mamhilad (Mamheilad)

Mammeliat (C12)[163], *Maimelad* (1254)[118], *Mamelar* (1291)[137], *Mamhilad* (1533-5)[164], *Mamhilod* (1577)[44].

Village 2 miles north north-east of Pontypool, former nylon spinning factory nearby. It is said that 'when Morgannwg was invaded by a force of English and Danes in 1022 A.D. the shrine of St. Cadwg was brought to the Monastery of Mammeliat'[163].

48

The name is from W *ma* 'place' or 'plain' and the personal name *Meilad (Meilat)*, a name occurring in the 'Lives of the Saints' so 'place of [or plain of] Meilad'.

Manmoel (Man-moel)

Ecclesiam de Mapmoil (1101-1117)[30], *Ecclesia Macmoilo* (C12)[165], *Mapmoil* (1102)[166], *Mapenoil* (C14)[167], *Mamm Howrell* (1631)[168], *Manmoel* (1840)[69].

Hamlet on Cefn Manmoel south of Tredegar. The C12 'Life of St. Cadwg' mentions *Ecclesia* de *Macmoilo* (from L *ecclesia* 'church' and the personal name *Macmoil* = *Macmoilus* i.e. 'Macmoil's Church') which is said to have been built by St. Cadwg for his disciple Macmoil[259]. This chapel, last mentioned in C14, has now disappeared.

The name Manmoel has come from the personal name Macmoil and in the forms Mapmoil and Mapen[m]oil the Ir *mac* 'son of' has become W *map* = *mab* meaning the same thing. Mapmoil and Mapenoil (from W *mab* 'son' W *pen* 'head' and W *moel* 'bald') means literally 'son of the tonsured or bald-headed one'. The form Manmoel is apparently an attempt to make sense of a name which had by then become difficult to understand. It has been derived from W *man* 'place or spot' and W *moel* 'bare or bald' but also 'a bare-topped hill'. This latter is currently a topographically accurate description of nearby Cefn Manmoel. But, as can be seen from the name-forms, this is in fact a late invention.

Markham

Former mining village north of Blackwood in the Sirhowy valley, Markham Colliery now closed. The Tredegar Iron & Steel Company started sinking a pit here in 1910 and this and the village which then grew up here took the name Markham from that of one of the Company directors, Sir Arthur Markham.

The somewhat remote village of Manmoel where once stood an ancient chapel (probably on Ty'r Capel Farm). The present chapel and burial ground is pictured here in 1950.

Marshfield (Maerun)

Maerun (c705)[169], *Mersfeld* (1291)[118, 170], *Meresfeld* (1295)[32, 170], *Meresfield* (1401)[171], *Marsshefeld* (1570)[172], *Mairin* (1535)[147].

Village on Wentloog Levels south of the main Newport-Cardiff road. Situated in a low-lying and formerly marshy plain. The name has been derived[170] from OE *merise* ME *mershe* 'marsh' and OE *feld* 'field' or 'open land'. This seems topographically appropriate.

The name Marshfield also occurs in Gloucestershire with similar name-forms i.e. *Meresfield* and *Mersfield*. But here the village so named is said to be situated on light land on a hill top! A derivation from OE *maeres* 'boundary' i.e. 'open country on the boundary' has been suggested for this Marshfield[173]. The same possibility exists for Marshfield on the Wentloog Levels. It is of interest that a nearby 'reen' or drainage channel is named *Pwllbargod Reen* from W *bargod* 'boundary'!

Michaelston-y-Vedw (Llanfihangel-y-fedw)

Sancto Michael (1254)[118], *Llanvedue* (1295)[32], *Lanvedue* (1314)[33], *Llanyhangel Veddo* (1577)[44], *Michelston Vedoe* (1614)[174], *Lanmihangel* (1254)[363], *Michelston* (1538-44)[364].

Village with church (from which the name is taken) north of Castleton, between Newport and Cardiff. The present name is a mixture of English and Welsh. In the English part, Michaelstone (from the personal name *Michael* and OE *tun* 'enclosure'- equivalent to W *llan*) is in effect 'Church of St. Michael'; Llanfihangel is the W equivalent. The W *bedw = fedw* means 'birch trees' giving 'the Church of St. Michael [amongst the birch trees]'.

Monkswood

Hamlet 1^{1}/2 miles east of Little Mill on Pontypool-Usk road. This was once a chapelry belonging to Tintern Abbey[178], hence the name. Iron smelting was carried on here on a small scale at a very early date (possibly by the monks).

Mynyddislwyn

Menedwisclelyn (1101-1117)[30], *Memt Eslim* (c1179)[175], *Menethestlyn* (1291)[137], *Menythystlewyn* (1478)[176], *Monethusloyne* (1610)[133], *Mynithisloyne* (1748)[177], *Ecclesia Tudor vab Hohele* (1536-9)[153].

Hilltop church, formerly with very large parish on ancient site above Ynysddu. The name is from W *mynydd* 'mountain' W *is* 'below' or 'lower' and W *llwyn* 'grove of trees', thus 'the mountain below the grove' or 'the mountain with the lower grove'. The name of a nearby farm Cae'r llwyn (from W *cae* 'field or enclosure' and W *llwyn* i.e. 'the field of the grove') points to the existence of a grove of trees hereabouts.

Islwyn was the bardic name taken (from Mynyddislwyn) by the noted Welsh poet Rev. William Thomas (1835-78) who was born at Ynysddu. It is also, now, the name of a Parliamentary constituency.

Nantyglo (Nant-y-glo)

Nant-y-gloe (1752)[179], *Nant y Glo* Works (c1790)[4], *Nantyglo* (1792)[180].

Village near head of the valley of the Ebbw Fach, above Blaina. There were early ironworks here (1795) and at nearby Coalbrookvale (1826) which took its name from Coalbrookdale in Shropshire, the 'cradle' of the iron industry. Coal mining was once important here but all mines are now closed.

A view overlooking Nantyglo in 1905, a period when it was an industrial heartland at the head of the Western Valley of Monmouthshire. The elegant dwelling in the centre was Nantyglo House, the home of the famed iron manufacturers the Crawshay family during the nineteenth century.

The name Nantyglo has come from W *nant* 'stream' and W *glo* 'coal' i.e. 'coal brook', probably indicative of coal deposits near the surface. Though the W equivalent of Coalbrook[vale] it was apparently in use before the latter name was introduced.

The name Nantyglo is found elsewhere in Wales e.g. Nant-y-glo, Mynydd Margam.

Newbridge

New Bridge (c1790)[4], *Newbridge Monythuscland* (1566)[365], *Newbridge* (1626-7)[366].

Town in Ebbw valley north of Abercarn, named after 'new' bridge over the river Ebbw, below Crumlin, once with two collieries (North & South Celynen). The lower part was once Trecelyn.

The name Newbridge is found elsewhere in Gwent (e.g. Newbridge on Usk, nr. Tredunnock) and in Wales.

Newport (Casnewydd-ar-Wysg)[181]

Novus Burgus (1138), *Novoburgo* (1191), *Neuborh* (1291), *Neuport* (1322), *Newport upon Husk* (1439), *Castell Newydd ar Wysc* (1172), *Y Castell Newydd* (C15).

Site of early church attributed to Gwynllyw (St. Woolos) the first ruler of Gwynllwg. The castle guarding the crossing over the Usk was the administrative centre for the medieval Lordship of Wentloog or Newport.

Once one of the great trading ports of South Wales and a major coal exporting centre. Unusual transporter bridge across the Usk. In 1839 Newport was the target of a Chartist uprising under the leadership of John Frost.

Name from L *novus* 'new' and L *villa* 'town' or from OE *niwe* 'new' and OE *burh* 'town' or 'port' i.e. 'the new port or town' (compared with the 'old' port or town of Caerleon).

A tug boat guides a freighter along the Usk and beneath the Newport transporter bridge. This photograph taken in 1905 shows the bridge still under construction.

The W form *Castell Newydd ar Wysg* means 'the new castle on the Usk'. In modern Welsh this is abbreviated to Casnewydd.

New Tredegar

Village at the head of the Rhymney valley, name originally White Rose (W *Rhos wen?*). A pit was opened here in the 1860s[160] which became known as New Tredegar Colliery (from Tredegar in the next valley) and the mining village which grew up nearby took its name from the colliery.

Nine Mile Point

When a tramway was being constructed in the Sirhowy valley in the early C19 the nine miles from Newport was built by the Monmouthshire Canal Company. The place where this section ended was known as Nine Mile Point; this later became the name of the railway station for Wattsville and the name was also taken by a colliery opened in the vicinity about 1905.

Oakdale

Village near Blackwood built by the Tredegar Iron & Steel Company to house colliery workers. Sinking the colliery began concurrently with house-building around 1907. A 'model' village was built and given the name Oakdale.

Ochr-Chwith

'Houses on a hill, across the Ebbw from Pontymister.' Name from W *ochr* 'side' and W *chwith*; this latter means 'left' but has also the connotation 'strange' or 'unusual'. *Ochr-Chwith* although near to Risca was once in the parish of Machen i.e. on the 'wrong' side of the mountain! On road signs *Ochr Chwith* has become *Ochrwyth* and *Ocerwyth*!

Panteg (Pant-teg)

Penteg (1254)[118], *Pentek* (1300-26)[182], *Pantege* (1585)[183], *Panteague* (1577)[44], *Panteke* (1404)[367], *Pant teg* (c1566)[280], *Panteg* (1790)[368].

Industrial village near Pontypool formerly with mines, foundries, tinplate works and quarries but also with historical associations; with a church on an ancient site.

The earliest name forms do not appear to make sense topographically; there appears to have been here a colloquial exchange of vowels (a→e) not uncommon in South Wales, the original name form being Panteg. This name may be derived from W *pant* 'hollow' or 'valley' and W *teg* 'fair' or 'beautiful' i.e. 'the fair hollow or valley'.

The name is found elsewhere in Gwent i.e. Twyn Panteg, near Machen.

Pantyreos (Pant-yr-eos)

Name of farm in Henllys district, also of reservoir supplying Newport. Name from W *pant* 'hollow' or 'valley' and W *eos* 'nightingale' i.e. 'hollow or valley of the nightingale'.

Pengam

Pengam Farm (1797)[184], *Pont ar Pengam* (1811)[185], *Pont Aber Pengam* (1836)[13].

Name of farm and of stream taken by colliery village in Rhymney valley, south of Bargoed. Also name of farm and of moorland at the mouth of the Rhymney river and farm name elsewhere.

W *pengam* means 'perverse, wrong-headed' but the place-name appears to have topographical significance. Pengam near the mouth of the Rhymney stands near a particularly sinuous stretch of the river so the derivation from W *pen* 'head or end' and W *cam* =

gam 'crooked' i.e. 'crooked end' seems appropriate. The colliery village Pengam is marked as Aberpengam on the first OS map, implying that the name has been taken from a stream and the same derivation appears likely.

Penmaen (Pen-maen)

Penmayne (1543)[186], hamlet of *Penmaine* (1709)[187], *Penmaine* (1752)[188].

Name quite common in Wales, often in coastal places, but here that of a village near Blackwood, once one of the hamlets of Mynyddislwyn Parish. At one time there was a Cistercian corn mill hereabouts. One of the earliest Nonconformist chapels in Wales was opened here in 1694.

The name is from W *pen* 'head or end' and W *maen* 'stone or block of stone' so 'stone headland'.

Pentwyn (Pen-twyn)

Kae penne Toyne (1564)[189].

This name occurs in a number of places in Gwent being that of small villages near Abersychan and Pontllanfraith, also of a hilltop village across the Ebbw from Llanhilleth. It is also the name of a number of farmhouses.

Name from W *pen* 'head or end' and W *twyn* 'mound, hill, hillock or rising ground' i.e. 'on top of the hill or rising ground'.

Pentwynmawr (Pentwyn-mawr)

Mining village between Newbridge and Pontllanfraith, on top of a steep slope above Newbridge.

Name from W *pen* 'head or end' and W *twyn* (as for Pentwyn) and W *mawr* 'big or great' i.e. 'on top of the big hill or slope'.

Peterstone Wentloog (Llanbedr Gwynllwg)

Ecclesia de Petro (1291)[137], *Lanbedr Gwynllwg* (1566)[190], *Peterston* (1577)[44], *Peterstone* (1618)[191], *Lampeder paroch in Low Wentllugh* (1536-9)[369].

Village on Wentloog Levels with church (from which it has taken its name); there was a monastery here in C12.

The W name is from W *llan* 'church' and W *Pedr* = *Bedr* 'Peter' i.e. 'Church of St. Peter'. The English name is again from the saint's name Peter and the OE *tun* 'enclosure' used here in the same sense as W *llan* i.e. again 'Church of St. Peter'.

Ponthir (Pont-hir)

Pontheere (1605)[192].

Village near Caerleon which grew up near an ancient ironworks (operating in 1800 when Archdeacon Coxe passed this way). Name from W *pont* 'bridge' and W *hir* 'long' i.e. 'long bridge', clearly from a bridge across the Afon Lwyd which preceded the present one (built 1800).

Pontllanfraith (Pontllan-fraith)

Tre pen-y-bont llynvraith (1492)[193, 195], *Tre penbont* (1502)[194,195], *Pontllynfraith* (1713)[195], *Pontlanfraith* (1783)[195], *Pontllanfraith* (1814)[195].

Large village just south of Blackwood in the Sirhowy valley at the crossroads to the Ebbw and Rhymney valleys.

The name-forms suggest that the *llan* in the present name was originally W *llyn* 'lake, pond or widened river'. The original name would then appear to be derived from W *pont* 'bridge', *llyn*, and W *fraith* 'speckled' which has been rendered 'bridge of the varicoloured lake'[195], (which seems odd). But what is meant by 'speckled lake' here seems to be a place where the river widens and where stones show above the surface (c.f. bara brith!); there is a place called Rhyd fraith (from W *rhyd* 'ford' some 3 miles to the south).

Pontnewydd

Pont Newydd (1638)[370].

Industrial village to the north of Cwmbran which has taken its name from a bridge over the Afon Lwyd. A tinworks was established here in 1802.

Name from W *pont* 'bridge' and W *newydd* 'new' i.e. 'new bridge'. Found elsewhere in Gwent.

Pontnewynydd

Ponte Thywonith (1602)[196], *Pont-y-duwinydd* (early C17)[197], *Pontnewynydd* (1792)[199], *Newynidd Bridge* (1843)[198], *Pontnewydd* (in error 1836)[13], *Pont Newinidd* (1697)[373], *Ponte ddewynith* (1664)[371], *Pont thewenith* (1661)[372].

Industrial village north of Pontypool. This name has been the subject of controversy and no satisfactory derivation has been advanced previously[200].

But the stream name Newynydd is also found near Crai, Powys and, most interestingly, the original form of this name is given by R.J. Thomas[201] as Dywynydd (or Dywenydd). Now W *duwinydd* in the name-form above means 'theologian or divine'. But it seems most likely that both *duwinydd* and *Thywonith* are, in

60

fact, variants of this same female name Dywynydd, the former being an attempt to give a meaning to an otherwise incomprehensible word. This then implies that the original name was indeed Pont Ddywynydd and the change of the second element to Newynydd (about which R.J. Thomas says some harsh words in the case of the other example) has taken place here too.

This implies that a stream running into the Afon Lwyd near Pontnewynydd once had the name Dywynydd. This stream name is found elsewhere in Gwent.

Pontrhydyrun

Pont Rhyd y Ryn (1644)[374], *Pont Rhyd ryn* (1701)[375].

Houses north of Cwmbran, site of tinworks established in 1806 (long closed). Name from W *pont* 'bridge' W *rhyd* 'ford' and W *yn[n]* 'ash trees' i.e. 'bridge of the ford of ash trees'.

Pontymister

Pont y mistir (1625)[202], *Pont y maister* (1624)[203], *Maister Bridge* (1635)[204], *Pont-y-maustre* (early C17)[205], *Pont y Meistr* (1836)[13].

Village south of Risca with bridge across the Ebbw from which it has taken its name. A derivation from W *pont* 'bridge' and W *meistr* 'master' i.e. 'the master's bridge' has been proposed locally.

But in medieval times a grange or monastic farm of Llantarnam Abbey known as Maister (Mayst') was in the vicinity[206] and this name appears to have come from W *mystwyr* 'monastery' (derived from L *monasterium*). The name thus means 'bridge of the monastery'.

An eighteenth-century drawing of the very first town bridge crossing the Avon Luyd in the centre of Pontypool and the buildings in the background still remain, close to the entrance to the park.

Pontypool (Pont-y-pwl)

Le Pool (C14)[167], *Pont poell* (1490)[207], *Pont-y-pool* (1680)[195], (1728)[208], *Pontypool* (1695)[209].

Formerly one of the principal centres of the iron and also the coal trade in the county, the town owes its origin to the ironworks started by the Hanbury family in C16. The Hanbury home, Pontypool Park, is now a Comprehensive School.

The earliest name form *Le Pool* is from W *lle* 'place' and E *pool* (from OE *pol* 'pond or pool') i.e. 'the place of the pool' (in the river, since Pontypool lies on the Afon Lwyd). The present name is from W *pont* 'bridge', i.e. 'bridge of the pool in the river'.

Pontymoile (Pont-y-moel)

Pontmoyl (1589-90)[210], *Pontmoel* (1640)[207].

Site of ancient ironworks, just south of Pontypool, in fact the first place in Wales where an ironworks proper was established; Richard Hanbury was in business here in 1576. Site also of a bridge over the Afon Lwyd.

Name from W *pont* 'bridge' and W *moel* 'bare hill or summit' i.e. 'bridge of the bare hill'. There is a bare hill nearby.

Pontywaun (Pont-y-waun)

Known also as Pontywain, houses north of Crosskeys in the Ebbw valley. A stone bridge once carried Hall's tramway across the valley to the Crumlin canal at this place although there may also have been an earlier bridge hereabouts.

Name from W pont 'bridge' and W *gwaun* = *waun* 'mountain pasture' or sometimes 'meadow', here, obviously, the latter i.e. 'bridge of the meadow'.

Rassau (Rasa)

Rhas-y-Mwyn (1697)[376].

Place north of Tredegar. Name from W *ras* 'race' (from E *race*) i.e. man-made watercourse to wash out iron ore.

Rhymney (Rhymni)

Industrial village at the head of the Rhymney valley which has grown up near the site of an ironworks (Union Furnace, 1801). Once there were collieries but these are now closed. The name has been taken from that of the river.

Rhiwderin (Rhiwderyn)

Rue yr derin (1622)[211], *Gwaun Rhiwderin* (1694)[212].

Village north west of Bassaleg. The name has been derived from W *rhiw* 'hill, slope or ascent' and W [a]*deryn* 'a bird' but this seems odd. A more plausible derivation is from W *deryn (derin)* which appears to be a diminutive form of W *deri* (plural of *dâr*) 'oak trees or oak grove' i.e. 'the hill or ascent with the small oak grove'. There is a parallel in Irish, Ir *doire* (derry) meaning 'oak trees or oak grove' and *doirin (derreen)* meaning 'little oak grove'[213].

The element *deryn (derin)* is found in other place-names e.g. Penderyn (near Hirwaun) and Twyn y deryn (near Nantyglo). 'Derreen' is a field name on the Machen Tithe Map.

Risca (Rhisga)

Risca (1146[214], 1230-40[114], 1535[215]), *Risca* (1600-1700)[216], *Riscae, Riskae, Riskay* (1600-1700)[216], *Riseley* (1577)[44], *Risga* (1779)[377].

This shows Risca in the last years of the nineteenth century. The famous 33-arch tramway bridge was demolished circa 1900.

Town in the lower Ebbw Valley, below the confluence with the Sirhowy at Crosskeys. Saxton (1577) gives the name as *Riseley* but this is clearly erroneous (the name appears as *Riskay* on a Saxton map of 1584).

The name Risca appears in two other localities in S. Wales: Nant Risca is the old name of the brook known as Nant-yr-Aber which flows through Abertridwr, and Cwm Risca (Risga) is the name of a small valley near Tondu, Bridgend.

The name of the latter is written *cwm yr isga* from W *cwm* 'valley' W *is* 'lower' and W *ga* = *ca* = *cae*. formerly 'hedge' then 'field or enclosure' i.e. 'the valley of the lower enclosure'. The name Risca has thus come from W *yr is cae* 'the lower field or enclosure'[216] where W *cae* has sometimes been pronounced and written *'ka'* (in south-east Wales). All three Risca names occur at the south ends of upland masses so the name is topographically meaningful.

Rogerstone (Ty du)

Tregwilym (C14)[167], *Rogerston* (1535[217], 1568[218]), *Rocheston* (1577)[44].

Once a village in the lower Ebbw valley, now part of Newport Borough. The Manor of Rogerstone was apparently given to Roger de Berkerolles who assisted Robert Fitzhamon in the Norman conquest of Glamorgan at the end of C11. A small castle was built here.

Name from the personal name *Roger* and OE *tun* 'enclosure' used here in the sense of 'farm' i.e. 'Roger's farm'. The W form of the name is from W *tre[f]* 'estate' and W *Gwilym* 'William' i.e. 'William's estate'. Roger de Berkerolles' father and grandson were both named William.

Before the growth of the present Rogerstone the northern part was known as *Ty-du* (from W *ty* 'house' and W *du* 'dark or black' i.e.

Once nothing more than a tiny village, Six Bells, Abertillery, expanded and developed rapidly during the latter half of the nineteenth century with the arrival of a busy coal industry. This photograph is from 1925 but bears little resemblance to the scene here today.

'the black house') and the southern part as *Tregwilym*. Both were then farm names.

There is a Rogerstone Grange near Chepstow (Rogeston 1291[217]); this was once a grange of Tintern Abbey.

St. Brides Wentloog (Llansantffraid Gwynllwg)

Sancta Brigida (1295[32], 1314[33]), *St Brides* (1572)[219], *Lansanfraed* (1676)[260].

Church and village on Wentloog Levels near Newport. The church is dedicated to St. Bridget (name contracted to St. Brides). The W form is from W *llan* 'church', W *sant* 'saint' and the personal name *Bridget = Bregit = Breit = Ffraed*. W place-names with *sant* 'saint' before the name of the saint are somewhat unusual.

Six Bells

Village south of Abertillery once with colliery. Name taken from local inn.

Sebastopol

Houses south of Griffithstown near Pontypool. Named by a John Nicholas who built some houses on this site; the name commemorates the siege of Sevastopol during the Crimean War.

Sirhowy (Sirhywi)

Village, once with ironworks, very near to Tredegar, at the head of the Sirhowy valley. The name has been taken from the Sirhowy River.

Swffryd

Sofrydd (1616)[220], *Soverith* (1707)[378], *Swffryd* (1882)[379].

Houses built on the mountainside above Crumlin. Name taken from that of three farms in the locality, Swffryd Fawr, Ganol and Fach; there is also a Craig Swffryd.

Name from the old W word *swf* 'spot or place' and W *ffridd* 'mountain pasture or sheepwalk' i.e. 'the place on the mountain pasture'.

Tafarnaubach

Near Tredegar. Name from W *tafarnau* (plural of W *tafarn* 'tavern') and W *bach* 'small' i.e. 'the small taverns'.

Talywaun (Tal-y-waun)

Tale y Wayne (1614-15)[380], *Tal-y-waen* (1707)[378].

Also Talywain, industrial village near Abersychan with ironworks built in 1826 for manufacturing iron bars from local ironstone.

Name from W *tal* 'end of' or 'head of' and W *gwaun = waun* 'meadow' or 'moorland pasture' i.e. 'end of the meadow [or moorland pasture]'.

Tanybryn (Tan-y-bryn)

Post-World War II Council Estate in Pontymister, below Fox Hill.

Name from W *tan* 'under or below' and W *bryn* 'hill' i.e. 'below the hill'.

Tranch (Y Transh)

Part of Pontypool, once with collieries and ironworks. Name (Y Transh) probably a form of ME *trench* 'ditch, cutting or track through woods'.

Tredegar

Tredegyr (C14)[167], *Dre-Degyr* (c1460)[221], *Tredegar* (1536-9)[153], *Tredegyr* (1570)[222], *Tredeager* (1577)[44], *Tredegar* (1787)[11], *Tredegar* (1568)[381].

Name originally that of the Morgan family estate (Tredegar Park) near Newport; Baron Tredegar created in 1859. Name then taken by the industrial town which grew up in C19 at the head of the Sirhowy valley on land belonging to the Tredegar Estate.

In medieval Wales, W *tre[f]* meant 'estate with a homestead and associated buildings' and place-names commencing with *tre[f]* followed by the personal name of the owner or occupier are quite common. *Tredegyr* thus appears to be 'the tre[f] of *Tegyr*' (a W personal name); the forms Tredeger and Tredegar which appeared later exhibit colloquial vowel variations which are quite common in South Wales.

Derivations from *tre deg erw*[223] 'homestead of ten acres' and *troed y gaer*[224] 'foot of the Gaer' have been proposed but these do not fit the name-forms and are on other grounds unlikely.

Tredegar is thus 'the *tre[f]* (or estate) of *Tegyr*.

Tredunnock (Tredynog)

Tredinauc (1254)[116], *Trefredinauc* (C12)[225], *Tredonauk* (1398-9)[382], *Tre Rydynog* (c1566)[280].

Village near Newbridge-on-Usk. Church reputedly a Norman foundation, Roman tombstone incorporated in walls.

A visit to Bedwellty Park in Tredegar will reveal two unusual relics from an industrial past, one of which is seen here. This is a lump of coal weighing an incredible 15 tons and intended for shipment to London's Great Exhibition of 1851, a 'much smaller lump', weighing just 2½ tons was hewn for the 1951 Festival of Britain.

71

Name from W *tre[f]* 'estate' or 'farm' and W *rhedyn* 'fern' with adjectival *'og'* i.e. 'farm or estate where ferns abound'.

Trefil

Trevill (1766-9)[383].

Small village near massive limestone quarries on minor road north of Tredegar, on Nant Trefil, overshadowed by the ridge Trefil Ddu.

The name of the latter has been rendered *Tir foel ddu* (from W *tir* 'land', W *foel* 'bare', and W *ddu* = *du* 'black or dark'[226]. However, the form *Tre[f] il* (c910) from W *tre[f]* 'estate' and a personal name occurs in the Llandaff Charters[227].

Trevethin (Trefddyn)

Throvetin (1254)[118], *Tref ddyn* (1535)[147], *Trevethin* (1612)[195].

Once the name of a small settlement with a church, reputedly founded by St. Cadwg, and a large parish, but now that of a suburb of Pontypool which has grown up in the vicinity.

The name has been derived from W *tre[f]* 'estate' and W *ddyn* 'fence' i.e. 'the fortified estate',[195] but a derivation from a personal name is possible; i.e. from the personal name *Meithin* (= *Feithin*). *St Meuthi[n]* was St Cadoc's preceptor; the *n* in the name may be a hypocoristic addition[384].

Troedrhiwgair (Troedrhiw-gwair)

Troed y rhiwgwair (1836)[13].

Place south of Tredegar, a long row of terraced houses, many now demolished, at the foot of a slope.

Name from W *troed* 'foot' W *rhiw* 'hill, ascent or slope' and W *gwair* 'hay' i.e. 'foot of the hillside of the hay'. Hay was formerly often cut on upland pastures.

Trosnant

Glin Trossnant (1537)[228].

Name of brook, also of the oldest part of Pontypool - on the opposite side of the brook to the early iron forges.

The name is from W *tros* 'across' and W *nant* 'brook' i.e. 'across the brook'.

Ty Isaf

Post World War I Council estate in Pontymister. The 6" OS map of 1886-9 shows a single farmhouse in this locality and this house was the source of the name, from W *tŷ* 'house' and W *isaf* 'lower', i.e. 'the lower house'. The Gwentian pronunciatin of *isaf* is 'isha'.

Ty Sign

The Signe (1654)[229], *Kaye nessa yr Signe* (1685)[230], *Tyr y Signe* (1760)[231], *Tyr y signe* (1797)[232].

Housing estate above Risca. The name has been taken from a small farmhouse once in the vicinity. But in earlier name-forms W *ty* 'house' is replaced by W *tir* 'land'.

A derivation from W *asyn* or *asen* 'donkey' has been suggested. But the second name-form listed i.e. *cae nessa yr signe* 'field near "the signe"' implies that 'signe' here is, indeed the English word 'sign' so the original meaning was 'the land with the sign'.

Signs were not infrequently displayed on dwellings etc. in C17 and C18; it is recorded that in 1706 in Newport there was a garden called 'The Sign of the Dolphin'[233]. But what the sign actually portrayed in the present case is not known.

Wattsville

Village in Sirhowy valley north of Crosskeys originally built c1884 to house workers at nearby Risca Colliery. Named after E.H. Watts, Chairman of the coalowners Watts, Ward and Company (then of United National Collieries).

There is a Wattstown in the Rhondda valley.

Wainfelin (Waunfelin)

Village on hill to north of Pontypool. Name from W *gwaun* = *waun* in this case 'meadow or moorland pasture' and W *felin* = *melin* 'corn mill' i.e. 'the mill on the meadow or moorland'.

Wyllie

Small mining village in Sirhowy valley north of Ynysddu. Built to house miners working at Wyllie Colliery, a pit sunk c1925 by the Tredegar Iron and Steel Company. Named after a Company director.

Ynysddu (Ynys-ddu)

Ynysddu (1715)[385].

Village in Sirhowy valley north of Cwmfelinfach. Site of small 'model' settlement founded in the 1820s by F.H. Moggridge (see Blackwood, Fleur de Lis).

Name from W *ynys* 'island or river meadow' (in this case clearly the latter) and W *du* = *ddu* 'black or dark' i.e. 'the black river meadow', Ynysddu is also a farm name in Mid. Glamorgan.

Ynysyfro

Name of farmhouse and of 2 small reservoirs (part of Newport's water supply system). Name from W *ynys* 'river meadow' and W *bro* = *fro* 'vale' i.e. 'the river meadow in the vale'.

Rivers and Streams

These include some of the oldest place-names in Wales; some are pre-Celtic in origin and interpretation is consequently often difficult. The classic work in this field is R.J. Thomas's 'Enwau Afonydd a Nentydd Cymru' of 1938.

Afon Lwyd

Avon (1314)[33], *Avon flu.* (1577)[44], *Afon* (1659[234], *Afon Llwyd* (1667)[234].

River flowing from Blaenavon through Pontypool and Cwmbran to reach the Usk near Caerleon. The early name-form Afon is from W *afon* 'river'; the second part of the name, from W *llwyd* 'grey' to give 'grey river' appears to have been added in C17, around the time of the Hanburys at Pontypool. At some time the river also appears to have been known as the Torfaen.

Big

Bige (1577)[235], *Byg* (1608)[236], *Beeg* (1616/17)[237].

Brook flowing into the Ebbw Fawr near Aberbeeg, once part of the boundary between the Lordship of Abergavenny and the Manor of Bryngwyn and Wentsland. Name possibly from W *pig* (plural *pigau*) 'point or spout'; the brook flows down between two sharp points of land to reach the Ebbw Fawr.

There is an Afon Biga near Llanidloes.

The Afon Lwyd whose source lies some two miles above the town of Blaenavon. Once known to locals as 'The Black River' due to unsightly pollution with coal dust, the waters are so much clearer these days as they flow to join the Usk near Newport.

Bran

Bran (1314)[33], *Nant Brane* (1634)[238].

Brook flowing from Upper Cwmbran to join the Afon Lwyd at Cwmbran. Name from W personal name *Brân* or from W *brân* 'crow'. The name is found elsewhere in Wales, e.g. Afon Bran near Llangadog, Dyfed and Nant Bran near Brecon.

Candwr Brook

A stream running into the Afon Lwyd in its lower reaches near Ponthir.

The name has been derived, romantically, from W *canu* 'to sing' and W *dwr* 'water' i.e. 'the singing waters'. But the name Camd[d]wr from W *cam* 'rounded, curving or crooked' is found in several places in Wales[239] and *'Candwr'* has probably been derived from this name, *'m'* having becoming *'n'*. Another example of a change of this sort is found in Cornwall.[240]

Carn

Brook flowing into the Ebbw at what is now Cwmcarn (see Abercarn). The name appears to have come from W *carn* 'mound, cairn or pile of stones' but also 'hill or mountain'; the latter being the more likely here. The rounded shape of the mountain Twyn Barlwm dominates the lower part of the Carn valley and is the likely source of the name (the mound on the top of Twyn Barllwm is a Norman motte).

A second much smaller stream running down the south side of Twyn Barlwm into Risca was also named Carn (i.e. *Nant-y-garn* 1720)[241].

A scene on the banks of the gentle river flowing through the Clydach Gorge. Whilst there are still some enjoyable walks to be taken in the valley, unfortunately much has been lost due to the development of The Heads of the Valley Road between Brynmawr and Abergavenny.

Celynan

Nant Colynan (c1790)[4].

Old name of stream flowing into the river Ebbw at Newbridge, down valley now named Cwm Hafod Fach on current 1" OS map. Name from W *celynnen* 'holly tree'.

Clydach

Cleidach (1779)[242], *Dyffryn Clydach* (1830)[242].

River flowing through the Clydach Gorge to meet the Usk near Gilwern; also the name of a number of other rivers and streams in South Wales. The earliest name forms of this group are *Cleidach*, *Clidach* and *Cloidach*. A derivation from Celtic **kleu* 'to wash' has been suggested[242].

Ebbw (Fawr and Fach)

Ebot, Eboth (1072-1104)[243], *Eboth* (1146)[244], *Ebboth* (1295)[32], *Ebbouith* (1536-9)[153], *Ebwith* (1577)[44], *Ebwy* (1694)[209], *Ebbw* (1833)[121].

The two streams Ebbw Fawr and Ebbw Fach meet near Aberbeeg then flow down the Ebbw valley through Crumlin and Crosskeys to the sea near Newport. The Sirhowy joins the Ebbw at Crosskeys. The name-forms listed appear to point to an original W *Eb[b]wydd*, *Ebwy* and *Ebbw* being late, contracted forms.

A number of derivations have been proposed, from W *eb* 'to speak' or 'to spring forth and gush' from W *ebol* 'colt' i.e. 'river associated with horses' or 'river wild as a horse' and from W *ebill* 'auger'. But the origins of this name are, in fact, unclear.

The Ebbw Fach purling through the park in Abertillery and just a mile or two before it joins the Ebbw Fawr at Aberbeeg.

Gwyddon

Nant Widdon (1710)[245], *Nant Gwyddon* (1830)[246].

Brook flowing into the Ebbw at Abercarn. A derivation from W *gwydden* 'wood or trees' has been suggested but seems unlikely (the entire area appears once to have been widely afforested). However, the W personal name Gwyddon (i.e. Gwyddon 'clergyman') appears as that of a witness to a transaction in the C12 Vita Sancti Cadoci[247] and this may be the origin of the name of the brook. The small brook *Nant Wyddon*[248] which flows into the Rhondda Fawr near the ancient monastic site of Penrhys may have acquired its name in the same way.

It is of interest that the old name of Trelleck Grange near Tintern was *Cil-wyddon* i.e. 'Gwyddon's retreat'[249].

Merddog

Small brook flowing into Ebbw Fawr near Cwm. Apparently once also known as *Mythve* (1779)[250, 316,] and *Myrdd fach*[386, 387]. Origin of name unknown.

Rhymney (Rhymni)[251, 252].

Remni (1101-1120), *Rempny* (1401), *Remny* (1536-9), *Rymney* (1541), *Rumney* (1755).

River once forming the western boundary of Monmouthshire, earlier of the old cantref of Gwynllwg. According to R.J. Thomas[251] the name has come from W *rhwmp* 'borer or auger' with the suffix *'ni'*, supposedly descriptive of the way the river erodes its course. On the other hand the name *Rhymhi* is found in the Mabinogion.

The church near the estuary (in what is now Rumney) *Ecclesia de Rempny* (1291) took its name from the river and the Cardiff suburb Rumney took its name from the church. The industrial village of Rhymney at the head of the valley, also took its name from the river.

Sor Brook

Soare (1622)[253], *Sore* (1677)[254].

Brook running from Llandegfedd Reservoir through Llandegfedd to reach the Usk above Caerleon. A derivation from W *sor* 'angry' has been suggested but the origin of the name is really obscure.

Sirhowy (Sirhywi)

Glynserny (1314)[33], *Sherwowe* (1476)[256], *Sirowy* (1508)[257], *Duffrin Serowy* (1536-9)[153], *Sroway* (1610)[126], *Sorwy* (c1790)[4], *Sirhowey* (1833)[121].

River flowing into the Ebbw at Crosskeys. Earliest name form somewhat uncertain ('n' and 'u' are not infrequently confused). A derivation from W *sor* 'angry' has been proposed though *Sorwy* is clearly a late form. The origin of the name is frankly unknown.

Syrowy (1650) is the old name of one of the upper tributaries of the Sor brook[258].

Sychan

Sychan (1616)[261], *Blaen Sychan* (1659)[262].

Brook flowing into the Afon Lwyd at Abersychan. Name from W *sych* 'dry' (indicating a tendency to dry up) and the diminutive '*an*'.

Tillery (Afon Tyleri)

Glenteler (1257)[121], *Teleri* (1332)[130].

Brook flowing into Ebbw Fach near Abertillery. Name from the W personal name *Eleri* or from W *ty* + *Eleri* = *Teleri*.

Tysswg (Tyswg)

Brook flowing into Rhymney at Abertysswg. Origin of name unclear.

Usk

The origins of the name have been discussed at some length (e.g. ref. 264). Although the Roman name Isca has clearly come from the British *isca* 'water' in the sense of 'river', Usk i.e. W *Wysg*, O.W. *Uisc* seems, in fact, to have come from the British **esca*, earlier **eisca*. This problem has not yet been resolved.

Ystrwyth

Small brook flowing into the Ebbw Fach near Blaina (formerly Aberystruth). A derivation from the W personal name *Ystrwyth* (ex L *instructus*) has been proposed[17].

References

Abbreviations

Arch. Camb.	Archeologia Cambrensis.
ASCM	'Apparitions of Spirits in the County of Monmouth and in the Principality of Wales', E. Jones, 1813.
BBCS	Bulletin of the Board of Celtic Studies.
BDD	Badminton Deeds and Documents
BLl.	'The Text of the Book of Llan Dav', J.G. Evans, and J. Rhys, 1893.
Cartae	'Cartae et alia Munimenta de Glamorgan', G. T. Clark, 1910.
CAPCW	'Calendar of Ancient Petitions Concerning Wales', W. Rees, 1975.
CAU	'Chronicon Adae de Usk (1377-1421)', E.M. Thompson, (1904)
Coxe	'An Historical Tour in Monmouthshire', W. Coxe (2 vols.), 1801.
CN	'The Charters of the Borough of Newport in Gwynllwg', W. Rees, (1951).
CPR	Calendar of Patent Rolls (1216-1334).
CClR	Calendar of Close Rolls (1227-1302).
CIPM	Calendarium inquisitionum post mortem sive Escaetum (1806, 8).
Daf Ben	'The Gwentian Poems of Dafydd Benwyn', J. Kyrle Fletcher, (1909).
DB	Domesday Book.
EACDW	'Episcopal Acts and Cognate Documents Relating to Welsh Dioceses', (1062-1272), J. Conway Davies, (2 vols.), 1948.
EANC	'Enwau Afonydd a Nentydd Cymru', R.J. Thomas. 1938.
ECPCW	Early Chancery Proceedings Concerning Wales, 1901 ff.

EGC	Earldom of Gloucester Charters, R. Patterson, 1973.
EHSWI	'The Early History of S. Wales Iron Works 1760-1840', John Lloyd. 1906.
EDST	'The Early Days of Sirhowy and Tredegar', O. Jones, 1969.
EL	'Enwau Lleoedd', Sir Ifor Williams, 1945.
EPCW	Exchequer Proceedings Concerning Wales, E.G. Jones, 1939.
Gabb	Baker-Gabb Collection, NLW.
GGG	'Gwaith Guto'r Glyn' I. Williams & J.L. Williams, 1961.
HA	'A Geographical, Historical and Religious Account of the Parish of Aberystruth', E. Jones, 1779.
HB	The Historia Brittonum, 3, The 'Vatican' Recension, D.M. Dunville, 1985.
HCMG	Historia et Cartularium Monasterii Sancti Petri Gloucestriae, Vol. 2, W.H. Hart, 1865.
HEV	'A History of Ebbw Vale' A Gray Jones, 1992 (rpt.)
HM	'A History of Monmouthshire from the Coming of the Normans to the Present Time', Sir J.A. Bradney, 1904-33 (4 vols.).
IPM (1295)	Inquisitio Post Mortem of Gilbert de Clare 2nd (C IPM p131-132), 'Edward 2nd in Glamorgan', Rev. J. Griffith, 1904, Appendix D, p.22.
IPM (1314)	Inquisitio Post Mortem of Gilbert de Clare (3rd) (C IPM p265-6), 'Edward II in Glamorgan'. Rev. J. Griffith, 1904, Appendix E p23.
IW	'The Itinerary in Wales' by John Leland in or about the years 1536-9' L. Toulmin-Smith, 1906.
JCH	The John Capel Hanbury Collection, GCRO, (3 vols.), 1955.
JFLT	Catalogue of Documents relating to the Jones Family of Llanarth and Treowen, GCRO (2 vols), 1967.
KT	Kemeys-Tynte Papers, GCRO.
LEA	Llandaff Episcopal Acta (1140-1287) ed. D. Crouch, 1985.
LBS	'Lives of the British Saints' S. Baring-Gould and J. Fisher (4 vols.) 1907-13
Ll.A	'Llantarnam Abbey, 800 Years of History', Sister Therese-Alphonse, 1979.
Ll.C	'An Early Welsh Microcosm; Studies in the Llandaff Charters', Wendy Davies, 1978.

Mil.D.	Milborne Family Papers and Documents, NLW.
MLSW	'The Marcher Lordships of S. Wales, 1415-1536 (Selected Documents)', T.B. Pugh, 1963.
MM	'The Mapping of Monmouthshire', D.P.M. Michael, 1985.
Mon.	Monasticon Anglicanum, W. Dugdale, 1846.
NCPNW	'Non-Celtic Place-Names in Wales', B.G. Charles, 1938.
NM	'Newport' Manuscripts, G.C.R.O.
NT	'The Valuation of Norwich',W.I. Lunt, 1926.
NTCB	'The Names of Towns and Cities in Britain', M. Gelling, W.H.F. Nicolaisen and M. Richards, 1970.
OE	'Old Ebbw Vale' by Keith Thomas.
OSM	Ordnance Survey Map.
PDR	Pontypool & District Review.
PM	Peniarth Manuscript 147, The Commotes and Parishes of Wales. Report on Welsh MSS no. 1 part 2, J.G. Evans, 1899.
PNDP	'The Place-Names of Dinas Powys Hundred', Prof. G.O. Pierce, 1968.
PNRB	'The Place-Names of Roman Britain', A.L.F. Rivett and Colin Smith, 1979.
PNT	Taxatio Ecclesiastica Anglicae et Walliae Auctoritate P. Nicholas IV, (c.1291), 1802 (ed.).
SBMR	Schedule of Badminton Memorial Records, NLW, 1965.
SCP	'Catalogue of Star Chamber Proceedings Relating to Wales'. Ifan ap Owen Edwards, 1929.
St. P & M	St. Pierre and Malpas Estates, Catalogue of Documents (Miss Protheroe).
SWB	Map of S. Wales and the Border in the 14th Century W. Rees, 1935.
SWMRS	South Wales and Monmouthshire Record Society (vols. 2,3 4), 1932.
TPM	Tredegar Park Muniments, NLW, 1950-86.
TPMD	Tredegar Park Muniments and Documents, 1950.
WJM	'Maesycwmmer, The Hidden Landscape' (1826-1939), Whitney Jones, 1989.
WPT	Williams, Price and Tweedy Documents, G.C.R.O.

1   PNRB, p 263.
2   HM 1. p 465.
3   TPM 46-57, p 728.
4   MM, pp 86, 87.
5   Ll. C, p 181.
6   VE 4, p 365.
7   TPM 1-45, p 716.
8   TPM 1, p 392.
9   MM, pp 100, 101.
10 'Monmouthshire Merlin',
      June 11, 1857.
11 MM, p 85.
12 EHSWI, p 157.
13 MM, pp 110, 111.
14 NTCB, p 37.
15 EANC, p 171.
16 TPM 1-45, p 119.
17 NTCB, p 54.
18 TPM 46-57, p 506.
19 ECPCW, p 223.
20 TPM 116-224, p 3126.
21 TPM 77-86, p 1520.
22 TPM 77-86, p 1528.
23 TPM 1-45, p 43.
24 TPM 46-57, p 503.
25 TPM 46-57, p 505.
26 TPM 1-45, p 162.
27 TPM 46-57, p 615.
28 'Y Geriadur Mawr', 8th ed.,
      H.M. Evans and
      W.D. Thomas.
29 Ll.C, p 137.
30 Cartae I, p 2.
31 VSB, p 128.
32 IPM (1295).
33 IPM (1314).
34 TPM 1-45, p 180.
35 TPM 1-45, p 284.
36 BBCS 7, (1935), p 277.
37 EL, p 10.
38 TPM 125-143, p 3591.
39 NTCB, p 49.
40 EHSWI, p 178.
41 'The Description of
      Pembrokeshire' by George
      Owen ed. Henry Owen
      1892-1936, 3, p 299.
42 BBCS 26, (1974/6), p 7.
43 TPMI, p 20.
44 MM, p 65.
45 MM, p 79.
46 EHSWI, p 145.
47 TPM 87-89, p 1759.
48 TPM 87-89, p 2242.
49 SCP, p 97.
50 MM, p 16.
51 'John Hodder Moggridge and
      the Founding of Blackwood',
      Pres. Mon. 25, 1968, p 25.
52 ECPCW, p 250.
53 'Dictionary of Place-Names in
      the British Isles',
      A. Room, 1988, p 43.
54 TPM 125-143, p 3591.
55 MM, p91.
56 NTCB. p 59.
57 NTCB, p 61.
58 PNRB, p 378.
59 TPM 46-57, p 716.
60 TPM 46-57, p 717.
61 TPM 46-57, p 721.
62 PNDP, p 125.
63 1W, vol.3, p 12.
64 'Oxford Companion to the
      Literature of Wales',
      M. Stephens, 1986, p 74.
65 TPM 125-145, p 3609.
66 TPM 1-45, p 177.
67 TPM 1-45, p 191.
68 Arch. Camb., 1849, p 120.

69 1st O.S. map, Sheet 36 (Cardiff), 1833.
70 'The Evidence of Place-Names', G.O. Pierce, Glamorgan County History Vol.2, Appendix 2, p 463.
71 PNDP, p138.
72 TPM 46-57, p 719.
73 TPM 1-45, p 9.
74 TPM 1-45, p 330.
75 HM 3, p 109.
76 TPM 1-45, p 240.
77 TPM 1-45, p 243.
78 TPM 125-143, p 3591.
79 TPM 1-45, p 189.
80 TPM 1-45, p 201.
81 TPM 1-45, p 25.
82 HM 1, p 288.
83 TPM 46-57, p719.
84 TPM 46-57, p 732.
85 Survey 'Manerium de Abercarne' (1631), Cardiff City Libraries MS. 4.476. p 47.
86 TPM 46-57, p 732.
87 MM, p 92.
88 EL, p 28.
89 MRCC Railway Timetable, 1857.
90 MM, p 103.
91 HM 1, p 472.
92 NTCB, p 80.
93 MM, pp 104, 105.
94 MM, pp 108, 109.
95 'Astudiaeth O Enwau Lleoedd Cwmwd Meisgin gyda sylw Arbennig Blwyf Llantrisant', R.J. Thomas, M.A. thesis, Cardiff, 1933, p 269.
96 PNDP, p 132.
97 TPM 77-86, p 1623.
98 CAPCW, p 287.
99 'The Origins of the Place-Names Fleur-de-Lys and Nelson', Beryl J. Toone, J. Gelligaer Hist. Soc. 4, 1967, p 11.
100 ECPCW, p 231.
101 MM, p 102.
102 ECPCW, p 1245.
103 HM 3, p 70.
104 TPM 87-89, p 1773.
105 TPM 77-86, p 1508.
106 TPM 1-45, p 240.
107 TPM 1-45, p 348.
108 TPM I, p 51.
109 TPM 46-57, p 808.
110 HM 3, p 113.
111 Ll.A, p99.
112 HM 1, p 464.
113 Ll.A. p 153.
114 EACDW, p 719.
115 ECPCW, p225.
116 TPM 1-45, p 69.
117 TPM 1-45, p 308.
118 NT.
119 ECPCW, p 232.
120 VSB, p 72.
121 MM, p 102.
122 Ll.C, p 115.
123 LEA, p 26.
124 SCP, p 108.
125 ECPCW, p 163.
126 MM, p 67.
127 EHSWI, p 198.
128 HM 1, p 359.
129 'The Myvyrian Archeology of Wales', 2nd Ed., 1870, p 756.
130 NTCB, p 37.
131 MM, p 83.

132 HM 3, p 359.
133 MM, p 68.
134 HM 3, p 250.
135 HM 1, p 464.
136 Arch. Camb., 1925, p 372.
137 PNT.
138 CAPCW, p 358.
139 HM 1, p 393.
140 MM, p 27.
141 HM 3, p 224.
142 ECPCW 2, p 656.
143 Ll.A, p 15.
144 1W, vol.5, p 8, Ll.A, p 210.
145 TPM 46-57, p 863.
146 Ll.A, p 19.
147 VE, Ll.A, p 33.
148 HM 3, p 127.
149 EANC, p 55.
150 HM 3, p 137.
151 EACDWD, p 719.
152 Cartae I, p 109.
153 1W, vol, 3, p 13.
154 MM, p 71.
155 EANC, p 163.
156 BLl., pp 207, 375.
157 Ll.A, p 102.
158 'The Daughters of Brychan',
    T. Thornley Jones,
    Brycheiniog, 17, (1976/7),
    p 22.
159 'Between Mountain and
    Marsh', J.A.F. Pickford,
    1946, p 126.
160 'The Place-Names of
    Glamorgan', H.C. Jones,
    1976, p 23.
161 NCPNW, p 239.
162 'Edward 2nd in Glamorgan',
    Rev. John Griffith, 1904,
    Appendix F, p 46.
163 VSB, p 111.
164 ECPCW, pp 230, 237.
165 Arch. Camb. 1932,
    pp 151-165.
166 Cartae I, p 719.
167 SWB.
168 Cardiff City Libraries MS.
    5 115, p 111.
169 BLl., pp 190, 341.
170 NCPNW, p 239.
171 TPM 103-115, p 115.
172 TPM 125-143, p 819.
173 'The Place-Names of
    Gloucestershire', H. Smith,
    3, p 59.
174 TPM 1-45, p 30.
175 T. Hearne's Appendix to
    'Adam of Domersham'
    (1727), p 604.
176 TPM I, p 13.
177 MM, p 76.
178 HM 1, p 71.
179 NTCB, p 138.
180 TPM 125-143, p 3591.
181 NTCB, p 141.
182 Ll.A, p 59.
183 TPM 1, p 869.
184 TPM 1-45, p 419.
185 TPM 125-143, p 364.
186 Ll.A, p 151.
187 TPM 46-57, p 730.
188 TPM 77-83, p 1701.
189 TPM 1-45, p 20.
190 'The Place-Names of Gwent',
    Canon E.T. Davies, 1982,
    p 29.
191 TPM 125-143, p 825.
192 HM 3, p 288.
193 TPM I, p 11.
194 TPM I, p 4.

195 NTCB p 152, BBCS 20, (1962/4), p 123.
196 TPM 77-86, p 1707.
197 'Handbook of the Geography and History of Monmouthshire' A. Morris, 1901, p 103.
198 'Apparitions of Spirits in the County of Monmouth and the Principality of Wales', Edmund Jones, 1813, p47.
199 TPM 125-143, p 3591.
200 PDR 4, (1973), p6.
201 EANC, p 140.
202 TPM 46-57, pp 712, 713.
203 TPM 1-45, p 268.
204 TPM 1-45, p 270.
205 SCP, p 193.
206 'Notes on the Place-Name Pontymister', G.O. Osborne, Gwent Local History, 1991, 70, p 27.
207 PDR 14, (1973), p 7.
208 TPM 1-45, p 2310.
209 MM, p71.
210 HM 1, p 433.
211 TPM 1-45, p 267.
212 TPM 1-45, p 276.
213 'The Irish Names of Places', P.W. Joyce, Vol.2, 1920, pp 503, 504.
214 Cartae I, p 130.
215 'Notes on Churches in the Diocese of Llandaff', C.A.H. Green, 1905, p 15.
216 'Notes on the Origin of the Place-Name Risca', G.O. Osborne, Gwent Local History, 1989, 67, p 3.
217 NCPNW, p 240.

218 TPM 1-45. p 168.
219 TPM 1-45, p 167.
220 HM 1, p 440.
221 Arch. Camb., 1884, p 35.
222 MM, p 27.
223 Arch. Camb., 1848, p 174.
224 Arch. Camb., 1848, p 372.
225 VSB, p 73.
226 'A History of the County of Brecknock', Theophilus Jones I, (1909), p 27.
227 Ll.C, p 183.
228 ECPCW, p 245.
229 TPM 46-57, p 74.
230 TPM 1-45, p 439.
231 TPM 1-45, p 74.
232 TPM 77-86, p 1673.
233 TPM 90-102, p 2303.
234 HM 3, p 223.
235 TPM 46-57, p 506.
236 TPM 46-57, p 512.
237 TPM 46-57, p 514.
238 HM 3, p 229.
239 EANC, p 46.
240 'Cornish Rivers and Streams', C. Henderson and H. Coates 1928 (See 'Gweek').
241 Cardiff City Library Documents, (1717-18), p 275
242 EANC, pp 8-12.
243 'Edward 2nd in Glamorgan', Rev. John Griffith, 1904, Appendix F, p 36.
244 EACDWD 2, p 637.
245 TPM 46-57, p 733.
246 EANC, p 114.
247 'Lives of the Cambro-British Saints', W.J. Rees, 1853, p 399.

248 Arch. Camb., 1906, p 284.
    p 3.
249 'Prehistoric Remains in
    Monmouthshire',
    T. Wakeman, Arch. Camb.,
    1906, p 284.
250 HM 1, p 472.
251 EANC, p 164.
252 NTCB, p 160.
253 HM 3, p 192.
254 HM 3, p 115.
255 'English River Names',
    E. Ekwall, 1928, p 374.
256 MLSW, p 93.
257 TPM 46-57, p 522.
258 EANC, pp 166-7.
259 VSB, p 128.
260 TPM I, p 786.
261 HM 1, p 440.
262 HM 1, p465.
263 EANC, p 87.
264 PNRB, pp 376-8.
265 Monmouthshire Review,
    vol. I, (1933), pp 386-406,
    vol. II, (1934), pp 51-57.
266 'Rhestr O Enwau Lleoedd' or
    'A Gazetteer of Welsh
    Place-Names', Elwyn
    Davies, 1967.
267 TPM 77-86, p 835.
268 JCH vol.2, p 155 (0136).
269 JCH vol.2, p 159 (0123).
270 TPM 506.
271 HA 15.
272 EPCW 257.
273 HM i 465.
274 EPCW (Ji) 257.
275 JCH ii 155 (0372).
276 SWRMS ii 102.
277 JCH i (100) (0430).

278 TPM 1764.
279 TPM 75.
280 PM 147, 920.
281 Coxe ii 247.
282 NT 54.
283 EHSW1 180.
284 TPM 495.
285 TPM 498.
286 TPMD 8.
287 MLSW 90.
288 JCH ii 185 (1410).
289 SBMR 40.
290 ASCM 19.
291 SBMR 50.
292 HB (Vat Rec.) 104.
293 DB 15, 1629.
294 EACDW i 26.
295 PNT 281.
296 GGG 140, 303.
297 MLSW 97.
298 TPM 136.
299 TPM 656.
300 Cartae i 38.
301 EACDW 79.
302 CPR 507, 508.
303 HM iii 281.
304 JCH i 128 (0351).
305 CN 6.
306 TPMD 13.
307 TPM 1600.
308 TPM 3609.
309 WPT ii 230.
310 TPM 7818.
311 NM 290 (1522).
312 JCH i 64 (1517).
313 MLSW 214.
314 JCH ii 113 (0527).
315 MM 111.
316 HA 14.
317 Coxe ii 252.

318 MM 92.
319 TPM 625.
320 NM 290 (6125).
321 JCH i 76 (0092).
322 JCH ii 224 (1567).
323 Mil D i 73, 74.
324 TPM 727.
325 JFLT 359.
326 MLSW 208-9.
327 Mon iv 633.
328 LEA 2.
329 MLSW 95.
330 TPM 1642.
331 MM 86.
332 EHSWI, 152.
333 HEV 56-7.
334 NM 320 (977).
335 Gabb 45.
336 JCH ii 179.
337 SBMR 49.
338 MLSW 219.
339 TPM 2475.
340 BLl 340.
341 TPM 2584.
342 TPM 3618.
343 JCH i 61a (1237).
344 JCH i 120 (1282).
345 JCH i 116 (0904).
346 JCH i 81 (1128).
347 VE iv 355.
348 EPCW 254.
349 BDD i 10.
350 ECPCW 163.
351 BL 320.
352 SCP 108.
353 NM 433 2 D43 (3714).
354 St. P & M 100 (D501, 549).
355 CCIR 366.
356 CAP 267 (7968).
357 VE iv 360.

358 NM 340, D43 5513.
359 JCH i 60 (0341).
360 WJM, 1989, 14/15.
361 EGC 146.
362 HCMG ii 63.
363 NT 325.
364 ECPCW 227.
365 TPM 1505.
366 TPM 1606.
367 CAU 40.
368 MM 87.
369 IW 19.
370 KT i 83.
371 JCH ii 160 (0187).
372 NM 350 (6535).
373 JCH ii 177 (0279).
374 JCH i 116 (0817).
375 JCH i 78 (0744).
376 EDST 30.
377 HA 42.
378 HM iii 235.
379 OSM 6 inch.
380 EPCW J 125.
381 Daf Ben 36 (46), 30 (50).
382 CIPM iii 235.
383 SBMR 33.
384 LBS iii 418.
385 JFLT 359 (D43 4799).
386 OE, Vol. 2 Plate 28.
387 OE, Vol. 3 Plate 26.

Abbreviations

ME	Middle English	L	Latin
OE	Old English	OW	Old Welsh
Fr	French	W	Welsh
Ir	Irish		

Also Available

THE PLACE-NAMES OF EASTERN GWENT

by GRAHAM OSBORNE
& GRAHAM HOBBS

ISBN 1 874538 91 3

The companion volume by the same authors which is
available from Booksellers or direct from
Old Bakehouse Publications,
Church Street, Abertillery, Gwent NP13 1EA